HOW COMPLEX IS TRINITY?

Dr. Maxwell Shimba

Shimba Publishing, LLC.

Shimba Theological Institute
Printed in the United States of America

TABLE OF CONTENTS

INTRODUCTION

The teaching about the Holy Trinity and the divinity of Jesus is one of the most perplexing topics for many people in the world of faith, not only for non-Christians but even for Christians themselves.

John 10:30-33 *"I and the Father are one."*

Then the Jews again picked up stones to stone Him. Jesus said to them, *"I have shown you many good works from the Father. For which of these works do you stone me?"*

The Jews answered Him, *"It is not for a good work that we stone you, but for blasphemy, because you, being a man, make yourself God."*

The Challenge from the Jews During Jesus' Time

As seen in this scripture, the Lord Jesus was attempting to reveal His authority to the Jews by explaining His relationship with the Father. Refer to His statement, *"I and the Father are one."* As a result of this declaration, the Jewish community became enraged, going so far as to decide to stone Jesus, accusing Him of blasphemy for claiming to be God.

Divergence of Understanding on This Issue, Groups, and Their Perspectives

1. **Ebionites** – They taught that Jesus was a mere human being and had no part in divinity, considering Him perhaps only as a prophet.
2. **Docetism** – This faith perspective held that Jesus was truly God but appeared as a human during His ministry and seemed to suffer. This philosophy derives from the Greek verb meaning "to seem" or "to appear."
3. **Arian Belief** – They believed and taught that Christ had some form of divinity but was ultimately a created being.
4. **Kenosis** – This doctrine, rooted in the teachings of the apostles, taught that Christ was fully God in every way but willingly laid aside His divine privileges and status to redeem humanity.
5. **Jehovah's Witnesses** – This Christian group has a completely different perspective from other Christians regarding the authority of Jesus. They argue that the doctrine of the Holy Trinity is unbiblical and a product of the Catholic Council of Nicaea. According to them, Jesus held an intermediate position between God and humanity, being the firstborn of creation but not God Himself.
6. **Muslims** – Islamic belief emphasizes the concept of the oneness of God (*Tawhid*), asserting that God is one and indivisible, without three persons. Therefore, they believe Jesus was merely a prophet with no divine connection. He performed great miracles as a human and a significant prophet sent by God, but there is no possibility of a single God existing in three persons.

Dr. Maxwell Shimba

Introduction to the Weight of the Challenge Regarding Jesus' Divinity and the Trinity

Dear reader, I trust this introduction provides you with an understanding of the complexity and significance of the challenges surrounding the divinity of Jesus and the Trinity as a whole.

Through this analysis, we will delve deeply into the foundation of this doctrine and its validity by examining the various aspects outlined in the introduction. Let us begin with the first section, carefully exploring the origin and basis of the Holy Trinity in the Bible. Welcome!

DR. MAXWELL SHIMBA

CHAPTER 01

THE ORIGIN OF THE HOLY TRINITY IN THE FOUNDATION OF THE BIBLE

There have been claims from various groups questioning the doctrine of the Holy Trinity and the divinity of Jesus, arguing that this doctrine may not be rooted in the Bible. Groups like the Jehovah's Witnesses claim that the Holy Trinity originated from the Catholic Church's Council of Nicaea, while our Muslim brethren argue that the doctrine's origin lies with the Apostle Paul.

In this section, we will begin a thorough Biblical investigation to uncover the truth about the origin of this doctrine and its scriptural validity. Without further delay, let us delve into the earliest Biblical writings, starting with the book of Genesis, to understand how God is revealed in the Bible.

Genesis 1:1-3 *"In the beginning, God created the heavens and the earth. 2 Now the earth was formless and empty, darkness was over the surface of the deep, and the Spirit of God was hovering over the waters. 3 And God said, 'Let there be light,' and there was light."*

In this passage from the very beginning of the Bible, the scriptures introduce the existence of God (*Genesis 1:1: In the beginning, God created the heavens and the earth*). Beyond merely describing the existence of God the Father, the Bible also mentions another Person, beginning with the *Spirit of God* (*Genesis 1:2: ...and the Spirit of God was hovering over the waters*). Following this, the next verse mentions the act of creation (*Genesis 1:3: And God said, 'Let there be light,' and there was light*), which essentially introduces the presence of another Person referred to as *the Word* as we compare with other Biblical passages.

Psalm 33:6 *"By the word of the Lord the heavens were made, and all their host by the breath of His mouth."*

In this verse, the prophet David shows that all things were created by the word of the Lord. However, in the New Testament, the Apostle John makes this authority even clearer, identifying it by name as we read:

John 1:1-3 *"In the beginning was the Word, and the Word was with God, and the Word was God. 2 He was in the beginning with God. 3 All things were made through Him, and without Him, nothing was made that was made."*

This passage reveals that the authority or Person involved in creation is referred to as *the Word* (*Logos*). To emphasize this truth, John explains that this Word has a heavenly origin, was with God, and was instrumental in the entire act of creation. Furthermore, it asserts that nothing was created without the involvement of this Person, the Word.

Summary

Thus, my dear reader, you can clearly see that the doctrine of the Holy Trinity has a genuine Biblical foundation. The Bible itself explicitly reveals the work of God through the three Persons, namely:

- **(God) – The Father**
- **The Word**
- **The Holy Spirit**

In addition to the passage from Genesis that we have studied, we can observe evidence of the work of multiple Persons of God in various other scriptures, further substantiating the truth and validity of this fundamental doctrine. Let us examine a few more passages from the revelations in the Bible. We will then extend our exploration slightly to consider whether extra-Biblical writings may offer insights similar to the Biblical perspective.

Genesis 1:26 *"Then God said, 'Let us make man in our image, after our likeness. And let them have dominion over the fish of the sea, and over the birds of the heavens, and over the livestock, and over all the earth, and over every creeping thing that creeps on the earth.'"*

In this first chapter of Genesis, we see God, considering His triune nature, speaking in plural form, saying, *"Let us make man in our image, after our likeness."* This provides the first additional evidence supporting the truth of the revelations and the work of the eternal triune God.

Consider this next scripture carefully:

Genesis 3:22 *"Then the Lord God said, 'Behold, the man has become like one of us in knowing good and evil. Now, lest he reach out his hand and take also of the tree of life and eat, and live forever—'"*

Here, the Bible recounts the fall of Adam and Eve, which led God to expel them from the Garden of Eden for fear that they might eat from the tree of life and thus live forever in a state of sin. To prevent this, God determined to remove them from the Garden. In God's statement, *"The man has become like one of us,"* we again see evidence of the revelation and work of God in more than one Person.

Let us examine yet another example from the same book of Genesis:

Genesis 11:6-7 *"And the Lord said, 'Behold, they are one people, and they have all one language, and this is only the beginning of what they will do. And nothing that they propose to do will now be impossible for them. 7 Come, let us go down and there confuse their language, so that they may not understand one another's speech.'"*

This passage recounts the story of early generations attempting to build a tower to reach the heavens under the leadership of Nimrod. This action angered God, who ultimately decided to confuse their language to thwart their plans. Refer to God's declaration: *"Come, let us go down and confuse their language so that they may not understand one another's speech."* This statement again points to the plurality of Persons, just as in the earlier declarations.

Thus, the Bible is exceedingly clear about this truth.

Descriptions from Other Religious Texts

I was greatly fascinated during my research on this topic to discover similar ideas in other religious texts. For example, the Holy Qur'an provides passages that present a perspective somewhat analogous to that found in the Bible, though Islamic scholars interpret these in a slightly different way. Let us review some of these passages from the Holy Qur'an:

Qur'an 22:5 *"…We created you from dust, your ancestor, Prophet Adam… then We continued creating you…"*

In this passage, the Qur'an attributes a statement to what is believed to be the voice of the one God. However, as seen in this verse, Allah uses the plural form when saying *"We created you from dust..."* This is quite similar to the Bible's Genesis 1:26, where God uses the same plural form, saying, *"Let us make man in our image..."* Therefore, both texts embrace the idea of plurality in divine speech. The division lies in the interpretation or rationale behind God using plural language in these statements. Each faith tradition offers its own explanation, as we will explore later.

Another example of such plural expressions in the Qur'an appears in the context of creation:

Qur'an 15:26 *"And We created mankind from dried clay of dark mud that had been molded."*

Here again, Allah is described using plural language in reference to the act of creation.

Let us also consider another instance of plural language in a different context:

Qur'an 4:154 *"And We raised the mountain above them (the Jews) as a sign of the covenant with them (to follow the Torah)..."*

In this verse, as believed in Islam, Allah again uses plural pronouns, saying, *"We raised the mountain above them..."* The phrase *"We raised"* reflects the same concept of plurality.

Comparative Observations

From these examples, we see that religious texts, both the Bible and the Qur'an, portray a similar depiction of God's work, as reflected through plural pronouns in divine statements. However, as mentioned earlier, there are differences in understanding the basis for this linguistic choice:

- **Christianity**: Christians interpret the plural pronouns as evidence of the triune nature of God, represented as the Father, the Word (Son), and the Holy Spirit, working in unity.
- **Islam**: Muslims maintain that Allah is strictly one in essence, indivisible, and without partners. They view the plural pronouns as a linguistic device to signify Allah's grandeur and majesty, rather than indicating multiple persons or a division in His being.

This divergence in interpretation is at the core of the theological distinction between the two faiths.

Christians – God is one, but in essence, He has revealed Himself in three distinct persons of operation. Thus, the use of plurality in divine speech unveils the depth and reality of God's nature, which is the presence of three persons within His unified authority: the Father, the Word, and the Holy Spirit—one Almighty God.

1 John 5:8 states: *"For there are three that bear witness in heaven: the Father, the Word, and the Holy Spirit, and these three are one."*

Dear reader, I trust that you now have a clearer understanding of the truth about God's nature based on the Biblical analysis I have provided. In this section, we have also observed how different communities present their perspectives on the concept of divine plurality. Our beloved Muslim friends, for instance, argue against the revelation of one God in three persons, asserting that it is impossible to derive one God from three persons and that such a belief would imply the existence of three gods.

While I will address this argument in the next part of my analysis, another claim worth addressing is the assertion that God cannot be divided and that when He uses plural expressions, it is merely a demonstration of His majesty or self-exaltation. Let us begin by addressing these significant points:

The Claim That God Cannot Be Divided

The answer to this claim is simple: it contradicts the descriptions of God in all religious texts regarding His power and authority. For instance, the Qur'an states:

Qur'an 57:3 *"He is the First and the Last, the Manifest and the Hidden, and He is the Knower of all things."*

This verse highlights the vastness of God's authority and power, concluding with the assertion that God is the Knower of all things. This implies that it is inappropriate to claim that there is anything God cannot do. He is omniscient.

The Bible also affirms God's limitless power, as God Himself declares:

Jeremiah 32:27 *"Behold, I am the Lord, the God of all flesh. Is there anything too hard for Me?"*

Thus, God has the ability to manifest and reveal Himself in any form or context if He deems it meaningful and beneficial in His role as the Creator and Sovereign ruler of heaven and earth.

Perhaps one of the key lessons we can learn as humans is that we should never impose limitations on God's actions or capabilities.

Explanation of the Claim: "God's Use of Plurality Is Merely a Sign of His Self-Exaltation and Arrogance"

The response to this claim is quite straightforward, particularly when we begin by examining a fundamental scripture. From there, we can delve into a brief explanation to resolve the issue.

John 13:13 *"You call me Teacher and Lord, and rightly so, for that is what I am."*

This verse in John provides a solid foundation for addressing this key claim. In His statement, Jesus aims to assure His followers of the validity and accuracy of the titles they use for Him, affirming that this is indeed who He is.

Jesus' statement, *"for that is what I am,"* demonstrates that God operates based on His true nature, not out of intimidation or self-aggrandizement that is inconsistent with His actual ability or essence. Therefore, it is challenging to agree with the notion that when God speaks in plural terms, it is merely to exalt Himself or to display arrogance without any deeper meaning in the use of such plurality.

Consider the following references:

Genesis 1:26 *"Then God said, 'Let us make man in our image, after our likeness. Let them have dominion over the fish of the sea, over the birds of the air, over the livestock, over all the earth, and over every creeping thing that creeps on the earth.'"*

Qur'an 15:26 *"And We created man from sounding clay, from mud molded into shape."*

In the Biblical context, these plural expressions attributed to God reflect or encompass the truth about His nature, specifically His eternal operation as three persons: the Father, the Word (Son), and the Holy Spirit—one God.

Refer to Jesus' own statement when commissioning His disciples. He mentioned the existence of these three persons and instructed His disciples to baptize in their name:

Matthew 28:19 *"Therefore go and make disciples of all nations, baptizing them in the name of the Father and of the Son and of the Holy Spirit."*

Analysis: Question 2

Can Three Persons Be One God?

This is a highly sensitive question and is likely the foundational reason why some people in the religious world reject this Biblical truth about the Holy Trinity and the divinity of Jesus Christ. The main objection in this regard appears to be mathematical, where those who oppose the Trinity argue that it is impossible for the Father, the Son, and the Holy Spirit—three entities—to constitute one God. According to this view, they contend that this is equivalent to saying $1 + 1 + 1 = 3$, not 1; therefore, Father + Son + Holy Spirit = three gods.

From this perspective, I must address the mathematical concept in more detail to determine whether such claims are valid and if they can be resolved philosophically within the scriptures.

Resolving the Issue with Scriptural Guidance from Isaiah

To address this matter, it is essential to let Scripture guide us, particularly through the following passage from Isaiah:

Isaiah 55:8 *"For my thoughts are not your thoughts, neither are your ways my ways," declares the LORD.*

This is a crucial reminder when engaging with this topic. In Isaiah, God makes it clear that His ways and thoughts are vastly different from human ways and thoughts. This truth is evident as we analyze the issue at hand, where the primary argument against the doctrine of the Holy Trinity is built on the notion that three persons cannot constitute one God because, mathematically, $1 + 1 + 1$ equals 3.

Examining the Mathematics (Three Persons - One God) in Scripture

Father + Son/Word + Holy Spirit = One God

The Biblical teachings and examples provided in the Scriptures clearly affirm the truth and validity of this fundamental doctrine in the realm of faith. To further clarify, the Bible explicitly presents the idea of one God derived from the sum of the three persons of God.

Unity in Plurality – Example 'A'

The first foundational evidence for one God in three persons comes from God's own statement in Genesis:

Genesis 1:26-27 *"Then God said, 'Let us make mankind in our image, in our likeness, so that they may rule over the fish in the sea and the birds in the sky, over the livestock and all the wild animals, and over all the creatures that move along the ground.'*

The first part of this passage shows God using plural language—"Let us make mankind in our image." Clearly, this statement reflects plurality. However, the plurality here signifies the expansive nature of God's actions as one God in three persons, not three separate gods.

This becomes evident in the next verse:

Genesis 1:27 *"So God created mankind in his own image, in the image of God he created them; male and female he created them."*

In verse 27, the language transitions from plural to singular, affirming that the plurality in verse 26 refers to one unified God. Thus, the use of "our image" in verse 26 and "his image" in verse 27 demonstrates that the Trinity reflects the unity and singularity of God's nature.

This analysis underscores the foundational doctrine that the Father, Son, and Holy Spirit are distinct yet one God, consistent with Biblical revelation.

Genesis 1:27 *"So God created mankind in His own image, in the image of God He created them; male and female He created them."*

Now observe this: the initial statement carried the concept of plurality when God said, *"Let us make mankind in our image."* However, the subsequent statement reaffirms God's unity by saying, *"So God created mankind in His own image."*

It is clear that these verses emphasize that the plurality or scope of God's actions exists within His unity and does not imply that the three persons constitute separate gods, thereby increasing the number from one God to three gods.

Understanding God in the Jewish Context – Israel

It is important to remember that, even during the era of the Jews, this was the understanding of God. The Jews referred to God as **"Elohim,"** a name that appears more than 2,602 times in the Scriptures. This name is a plural form of the word **"El" (God),** carrying the concept of plurality within unity.

Despite this understanding, the Jewish perspective remained firmly rooted in the truth of one God only. This concept was central to their faith and was enshrined in their **monotheistic** belief system. The term "monotheistic" comes from the Greek words **"mono"** (one) and **"theistic"** (God). This idea of one God is firmly established in the

Bible through a passage that the Jewish community calls the **Shema**, a Hebrew word meaning *"Hear"*:

Deuteronomy 6:4 *"Hear, O Israel: The LORD our God, the LORD is one."*

Through this verse, the Jewish people built an unshakeable foundation of faith in the one God.

However, it is also important to note that this belief in one God took into account God's eternal nature and the work of His three persons, as previously discussed. Even in the Shema (Deuteronomy 6:4), the oneness of God is emphasized through the phrase *"The LORD is one."* The Hebrew word used for *"one"* is **"Echad,"** which signifies *"a united one."*

The Concept of Unity Within Plurality

The term **"Echad"** (one/united) supports the idea of unity within plurality. This same word is used to describe the unity in the bond of marriage between a man and a woman, as seen in:

Genesis 2:24 *"That is why a man leaves his father and mother and is united to his wife, and they become one flesh (Echad)."*

The word *"one"* in this verse is translated from the same Hebrew word **"Echad"** that is used to explain the unity of God. This indicates that the concept of unity here arises from the union of more than one entity and reflects the expansive work of God's multiple persons.

Further Scriptural Evidence of Unity in Three Persons

To continue addressing this question, let us examine additional Biblical examples that demonstrate the possibility of three persons being one God. As noted earlier, the critique of this doctrine often focuses on the mathematical notion of whether $1 + 1 + 1$ can equal 1. Let us now explore further scriptural evidence to provide clarity and establish the foundational truth of unity within the Trinity.

The Unity of God in Three Persons: Part B

2 Peter 3:8 *"But do not forget this one thing, dear friends: With the Lord a day is like a thousand years, and a thousand years are like a day."*

This scripture is crucial in addressing the argument that approaches the concept of the Trinity mathematically. Just as the argument itself is mathematical in nature, Peter's statement dismantles that notion by demonstrating that God's calculations are vastly different from human calculations. What may appear as a multitude to us, as human beings, is not a multitude to God. Refer again to the latter part of 2 Peter 3:8: *"…With the Lord a day is like a thousand years, and a thousand years are like a day."*

To make it easier to resolve our argument, we can slightly reframe these words by saying: *"With the Lord, one God is like three persons, and three persons are like one God."*

It is my belief, dear reader, that through this analogy, you are beginning to gain clarity on this matter. As we proceed with this analysis, examining additional scriptures and examples, I trust that any doubts you may have about understanding this essential doctrine of faith will be resolved.

THE TRINITY IS PROVED BY BIBLE VERSES AND MATHEMATICS

Let's start by reading the verse:

1 John 5: 7 *For there are three that bear record in heaven, the Father, the Word, and the Holy Ghost: and these three are one.*

The Bible verse says:

THERE ARE THREE: $1 + 1 + 1 = 3$

1. Father
2. Word - Jesus
3. The Holy Spirit
These Three are witnessing in Heaven.

THESE THREE ARE ONE: $1 * 1 * 1 = 1$

GOD IS ETERNAL:

∞ INFINITY

Psalm 90: 2 tells us about God's eternal life: "Before the mountains were brought forth, or ever thou hadst formed the earth and the world, even from everlasting to everlasting, thou art God." Since humans measure everything over time, it is very difficult for us to conceive of something that has no beginning, but has always been, and will continue forever.

1. The Father is Eternal: He Has No Beginning or End ∞
2. The Son Is Eternal: He Has No Beginning or End ∞
3. The Holy Spirit is Eternal: He Has No Beginning or End ∞

JESUS IS ETERNAL ∞

Jesus Christ, the God of the flesh, also affirmed His divinity and eternal life to the people of His day by saying, "Before Abraham was born, I am" (John 8:58). It is clear that Jesus was claiming to be God in the flesh because the Jews, when they heard these words, tried to stone him. To the Jews, proclaiming the eternal God was blasphemous and worthy of death (Leviticus 24:16). Jesus was claiming to be eternal, just as his Father is eternal. The apostle John also proclaimed this truth about the nature of Christ: "In the beginning was the Word, and the Word was with God, and the Word was God" (John 1: 1). Jesus and his Father are one and the same, when they have no time, and they share equally in eternal glory.

THE HOLY SPIRIT IS ETERNAL ∞

Spirit of God / Lord / Christ: (Matthew 3:16, 2 Corinthians 3:17, 1 Peter 1:11) These names remind us that the Spirit of God is indeed part of the Triune God and that He is equal with God as Father. and the Son. He first reveals us at the time of creation, when he "walked on the water," signifying his role in creation, as well as that of Jesus who "made all things" (John 1: 1-3). We see that Trinity of God again at the baptism of Jesus, when the Spirit descends upon Jesus and the voice of the Father is heard.

NOW LET US USE MATHEMATICS:

Eternity in Mathematics is indicated by this symbol ∞. In English they say it is "INFINITY"

Using basic Mathematics, you will see $\infty + \infty + \infty = \infty$

FATHER ∞ + SON ∞ + HOLY SPIRIT ∞ = ∞

$1 + 1 + 1 = 3$ There are Three who bear witness in Heaven: There are THREE that bear witness in heaven.

$1 \times 1 \times 1 = 1$ These Three Are One: These THREE ARE ONE

$$\infty + \infty + \infty = \infty$$

God the Father has no beginning or end: The Father has no beginning or end = ETERNAL = ∞

Word-Jesus has no Beginning or End:

The Word "Jesus" has no beginning or end = ETERNAL = ∞

The Holy Spirit has no beginning or end: The Holy Spirit has no beginning or end = ETERNAL = ∞

Now I put the paragraph again:

1 John 5: 7 For there are three that bear record in heaven, the Father, the Word, and the Holy Ghost: and these three are one. For there are three that bear witness in heaven: the Father, the Word, and the Holy Spirit; and these THREE ARE ONE. ~ 1 John 5: 7

SUMMARY

On the subject of the TRINITY, it involves the NUMBER THREE and so its rule must be "TERNARY ADDITION" and not "BASE TEN ADDITION" as many of you use that calculation without even realizing that in addition you are applying the BASE TEN LAW.

NOW WHAT DOES TERNARY ADDITION MEAN:

1. Ternary number uses BASE 3, as opposed to BASE 10 which if you count and reach number 9, you go back to 1 and add "ZERO" = 10. NOW, in Ternary addition, when you count the number you end up with TWO and the next is 10, as in "BINARY ADDITION" your last number is ONE http://www.allaboutcircuits.com/.../d.../chpt-2/binary-addition/.

I know many of you have probably never learned Higher Mathematics, but log in here and learn for yourself Ternary addition
http://homepage.cs.uiowa.edu/~jones/ternary/arith.shtml

NOW LET'S START CONFIRMING THE TRINITY OF GOD THROUGH NUMBERS

TERNARY ADDITION BASIS APPLICABLE:

A. (1 + 1 + 1) Ternary = 10 Ternary

YOU SEE, YOUR ANSWER IS Ternary (10)

NOW our numbers have been reduced to Ternary 10. now, let us break "10" by adding 1 + 0 while using ternary addition

B. (1 + 0) Ternary = 1 Ternary.

ACCORDINGLY, THE TRINITY IS PROVABLE BY USING MATHEMATICS, and today I have answered all those whose MATHEMATICS IS NOT THEIR SUBJECT that THE TRINITY IS PROVABLE EVEN BY USING MATHEMATICS.

NOW GO AND ASK YOUR MATHEMATICS TEACHER THE FOLLOWING:

A. Ternary of (1 + 1 + 1) =?

B. Ternary of (1 + 2) =?

AFTER YOU RECEIVED THE ANSWER, ASK YOUR TEACHER AGAIN

C. Ternary of (1 + 0) =?

GOD IS IMPECCABLY THE FOUNDER OF MATHEMATICS and nothing is impossible.

God bless you so much, and today YOU HAVE BEEN ANSWERED THAT THE TRINITY IS PROVABLE EVEN IN MATHEMATICS.

SATISFIED WITH WHAT WE HAVE REVEALED.

A. THE FATHER is called GOD (1 CORINTHIANS 8: 6).

B. THE SON (JESUS) is called GOD (ISAIAH 9: 6; JOHN 20: 26-29).

C. THE HOLY SPIRIT IS CALLED GOD (ACTS 5: 3-4)

In Isaiah 48:16 and 61: 1, the Son speaks while associating the Father with the Holy Spirit. Compare Isaiah 61: 1 with Luke 4: 14-19 to see the Son speaking. Matthew 3: 16-17 describes the baptism of Jesus. Appearing here is God the Holy Spirit descending on God the Son, God the Father declaring His joy in the Son. Matthew 28:19 and 2 Corinthians 13:14 are examples of three persons in one God.

CHAPTER 02

THE UNITY OF MULTIPLE ELEMENTS PRODUCING ONE "PLURALITY IN UNITY"

'The Unity of Multiple Elements Producing One' (Plurality in Unity)

The Bible offers various examples of how a combination of more than one element can result in a singular entity, as illustrated in the following verses:

Genesis 1:5 *"God called the light 'day,' and the darkness he called 'night.' And there was evening, and there was morning—the first day."*

This verse explains the principle behind the formation of a "day"—it is the union of evening (darkness) and morning (light) that constitutes one day, not two.

Similarly, it would be incorrect to claim that the unity of the three persons of God results in three gods while we accept that one day, formed by the union of two elements, is still called one day.

Let us do this calculation:
Evening + Morning = One Day (Genesis 1:5)
Now consider this:
Father + Son + Holy Spirit = One God (1 John 5:8)
I trust that this brings greater clarity to the matter, dispelling doubts and concerns. Let us examine another example:

Ezekiel 37:17 *"Join them together into one stick so that they will become one in your hand."*

In this instruction, God tells the prophet Ezekiel to take two sticks and join them so they become one stick in his hand.

This emphasizes the possibility of unity arising from the combination of multiple elements, yet resulting in one entity. Thus, the notion that the three persons of God cannot constitute one God is entirely negated by these biblical examples.

Simple Analogies

The Trinity in an Egg If you take a boiled egg and peel it, you will find that it contains three distinct parts: the hard outer shell, the soft white albumen, and the yolk. Despite having these three components, no one would argue that the egg is three separate eggs. Instead, we all recognize it as one egg with three elements within it.

This simple analogy helps us comprehend and accept the profound truth of the Holy Trinity.

Two Lenses from One Eye

In another analogy often used in my sermons, I liken the unity of the Trinity to the human eye. When asked how they see, most people respond that their vision comes from having two eyes. However, if asked to look left and right simultaneously, they find it impossible.

This shows that human sight originates from a single source of vision, even though God has given us two lenses for a broader field of view. The control or source of sight is still one.

These examples simplify the complex concept of unity within plurality, making it easier to believe in and understand the true and sound doctrine of the Holy Trinity.

Therefore, One God Can Reveal Himself in More Than One Person Yet Remain One God While Acting Within a Broader Scope of Authority

The World of the Trinity

It amazes me personally how Almighty God has embedded abundant evidence of the Trinity even within the scientific and geographical structures of the universe. I fear that those who oppose this doctrine may find themselves judged by science itself on the Day of Judgment for the irrationality of their opposition.

Consider how various scientific and geographical domains are dominated by indicators or evidence of the Trinity:

- To form a *world*, there is a union of **Earth + Air + Sky**.
- To form a *universe*, there is a union of **Mass + Space + Time**.
- To form an *atom*, there is a union of **Proton + Electron + Neutron**.
- To form *time*, there is a union of **Past + Present + Future**.
- To form a *sphere*, there is a union of **Lithosphere + Hydrosphere + Atmosphere**.
- To form a *number*, there is a union of **Positive + Zero + Negative**.
- To form *air*, there is a union of **Nitrogen + Oxygen + Water Vapor**.
- To form *water*, there is a union of **Hydrogen (x2) + Oxygen**.
- To form *music*, there is a union of **Melody + Harmony + Rhythm**.

From these observations, it is evident that the philosophy of the Trinity pervades much of geography and creation as a whole. Personally, I see this as strong evidence supporting the truth of the Holy Trinity. It also serves as a practical response to the argument that unity cannot arise from plurality.

The Holy Trinity in the Worship of Heavenly Beings
Another strong piece of evidence that concludes this analysis is found in the worship system of heavenly beings.

Their declarations clearly affirm the foundation of God's Trinity. Let us examine the following scripture:

Revelation 4:8 *"Each of the four living creatures had six wings and was covered with eyes all around, even under its wings. Day and night they never stop saying: 'Holy, holy, holy is the Lord God Almighty,' who was, and is, and is to come."*

This biblical passage vividly illustrates the worship in heaven. The declarations of these heavenly beings affirm the Trinity of God by repeating *Holy* three times: *Holy, Holy, Holy, Lord God Almighty, who was, and is, and is to come.*

Not only do they proclaim "Holy" three times, but they also specify the characteristics of the persons within the Trinity:

- *Who was* refers to God the Father.
- *Who is* refers to the Holy Spirit, who presently reigns.
- *Who is to come* refers to Jesus, who the world awaits for His second coming, as heaven also anticipates His return to earth after completing His work of mediation in the heavenly temple.

May God bless you as you renew your understanding, having gained this foundational explanation supported by the evidence of God's Word.

(Analysis, Question No. 3)

How Does the Lord Jesus Become God?

After gaining a clear understanding of the concept of one God existing in three persons, it is fitting to take another step forward by addressing this critical question. This question often stirs significant confusion among many in the world of faith. The root of the confusion lies in understanding the truth about the divine origin of the Lord Jesus, leading many to question, *How does Jesus become God?*

The question fundamentally seeks to uncover the source or origin of Jesus' divine authority, especially considering His earthly appearance, which suggests that He may have had a worldly origin. To provide a foundational answer, it is essential to first examine the nature of Jesus before delving deeper into understanding the truth of His divinity.

Understanding the Nature of Jesus

The significant opposition from the Pharisees and some Jews regarding the divinity of Jesus stemmed from their misunderstanding of His nature. Many Jews' perception was limited to Jesus' human appearance and His earthly lineage through Mary. As a result, the Jews at one point said:

John 6:42 *"They said, 'Is this not Jesus, the son of Joseph, whose father and mother we know? How can he now say, "I came down from heaven"?'"*

This passage sheds light on the root of the issue. The Jews' main argument was that it was improper for Jesus to claim

He came down from heaven since they knew He was born of Mary and His father was Joseph, making His origin purely earthly.

This perspective made it difficult for them to accept Jesus' declarations of having a heavenly origin, which became the primary source of their opposition to His statements. Consider another instance of their argument when Jesus spoke of His eternal existence:

John 8:56-58 *"Your father Abraham rejoiced at the thought of seeing my day; he saw it and was glad."* The Jews replied, *"You are not yet fifty years old, and you have seen Abraham?"* Jesus answered, *"Very truly I tell you, before Abraham was born, I am!"*

In this scripture, the Jews opposed Jesus' statement, which implied a direct relationship and connection with Abraham. They questioned Him, arguing that as a young man not yet fifty years old, it was impossible for Him to have seen Abraham. In response, Jesus boldly stated that His existence preceded Abraham's: *"Before Abraham was born, I am."*

From my perspective, the core issue for the Jews—and those who oppose the divinity of Jesus due to His humanity or His birth by Mary—is not primarily His earthly origin. Rather, it is their failure to grasp the fundamental truth about Jesus' preexistence before His birth by Mary.

What Is the Origin of Jesus?

To answer this question, the Lord Jesus Himself frequently educated the Jews about the truth of His origin. He sought to help them move away from viewing Him solely as a person of earthly origin and instead to recognize that He existed before coming to earth as a human for the purpose of redeeming humanity. Consider these scriptures carefully:

John 8:23 *"But he continued, 'You are from below; I am from above. You are of this world; I am not of this world.'"*

John 6:62 *"Then what if you see the Son of Man ascend to where he was before?"*

From these verses, Jesus explicitly highlights His heavenly origin, affirming that His existence transcends the earthly realm. This teaching demonstrates that His humanity does not negate His divinity, but rather, His coming in human form was a purposeful act for humanity's salvation.

In both of these scriptures, the Lord Jesus clearly and unequivocally asserts His heavenly origin before becoming human and being born of Mary. In the first passage, Jesus highlights a distinct difference between Himself and ordinary humans by saying: *"You are from below; I am from above. You are of this world; I am not of this world."*

In the other statement, Jesus challenges the Jews by asking: *"What if you see the Son of Man ascend to where He was before?"* This indicates that before His earthly appearance, He already existed somewhere (in heaven).

The Origin of Jesus and the Foundation of His Divinity

Understanding the origin of Jesus becomes straightforward given the strong foundation we've established from the beginning of this analysis, especially through Jesus' own declarations. These statements present a clear picture that Jesus never had an earthly, human origin, despite being born of Mary. His birth through Mary was not the beginning of His existence but rather a means to veil His divine authority so He could reach humanity, as we will explore further.

Moreover, the natural principles that define human origin did not apply to Jesus in the process of His birth. Let us examine this scripture:

Matthew 1:18 *"This is how the birth of Jesus the Messiah came about: His mother Mary was pledged to be married to Joseph, but before they came together, she was found to be pregnant through the Holy Spirit."*

The birth of Jesus stands in stark contrast to the ordinary biological principles of human reproduction. According to this scripture, the Bible explicitly states that Mary conceived Jesus before coming together with a man, and the conception was by the power of the Holy Spirit.

A Unique Birth, Outside Human Reproductive Systems

In Jesus' birth, there was no involvement of the natural biological processes that encompass scientific reproductive stages. For instance, even the Qur'an outlines the stages of human creation in one of its chapters, as seen below:

Qur'an 22:5 *"O mankind! If you are in doubt about the Resurrection, then (consider this): We created you from dust (your forefather, Prophet Adam), then from a drop of sperm (the seed of life), ..."*

The Qur'an here clearly explains these stages of creation, identifying them as principles used to create humans and propagate their lineage. These two methods include the initial creation from dust (Adam and Eve) and the method of reproduction through sperm (subsequent human beings).

Jesus was born during a time when the natural system for human reproduction required two individuals of opposite sexes to engage in sexual union, leading to conception. The mother would then carry the pregnancy for nine months before giving birth, as science extensively explains:

"Sexual reproduction is a process that creates a new organism by combining the genetic material of two organisms; this is followed by an exchange of genetic information (a process called genetic recombination). After the new recombinant chromosome is formed, it is passed on to progeny."

Sexual reproduction involves the creation of a new being through the union of reproductive cells from two living organisms. This is followed by the exchange of genetic information, a process known as *genetic recombination.*

Once the new genetic material is formed, it passes through female reproductive hormones, facilitating conception in the uterus and nurturing the embryo, with various stages culminating in the birth of the being.

However, in the case of Jesus, none of these natural reproductive stages were involved. His conception was entirely divine, carried out through the Holy Spirit, marking His birth as supernatural and distinct from ordinary human births. This divine conception underscores His unique origin and further establishes the foundation of His divine authority.

Therefore, in general, other beings come into existence through the principle of the union of reproductive cells from both genders—that is, from the father and the mother—a process that never occurred in the birth of the Lord Jesus. This raises profound reflection on His origin and, above all, His authority.

In this section, we will delve directly into foundational scriptures to gain a complete understanding of the origin and authority of the Lord Jesus. To begin, it is appropriate to establish this foundation through the words of the Apostle John:

John 1:1-2

"In the beginning was the Word, and the Word was with God, and the Word was God. He was with God in the beginning."

It becomes clear, dear reader, that you can now begin to see the light after reading this passage from the Gospel of John. The Apostle John, with the help of the Holy Spirit, explicitly reveals the foundation of Jesus' origin, identifying the Lord Jesus as the *Word* who existed in heaven and, fundamentally, was the agent of all creation.

If you recall from earlier, dear reader, we discussed at length God's work in the unity of the three eternal Persons of the one God. Among these Persons is the Word (the Son).

In this context, the Apostle John explicitly identifies the Word as the Lord Jesus Himself before He became human. Refer to verse 14 of John chapter 1:

John 1:14

"The Word became flesh and made His dwelling among us. We have seen His glory, the glory of the one and only Son, who came from the Father, full of grace and truth."

This verse clearly identifies the Word as Jesus, who eventually became flesh and lived among us. His glory, as the one and only Son from the Father, was revealed to us. (We will elaborate on this further.)

Jesus' Preexistence and Divine Authority

The Bible explicitly affirms that the Lord Jesus existed before the creation of this world. If you are a diligent Bible reader, you will notice that even Jesus Himself made several statements emphasizing His preexistence in heaven as part of God's unity and as the Word. Let us read this verse together:

John 17:5

"And now, Father, glorify Me in Your presence with the glory I had with You before the world began."

Here, the Lord Jesus openly declares that He existed before the creation of the world. More importantly, He reveals that He shared in the glory and unity of work and ownership with the Father. This statement aligns perfectly with another instance where Jesus spoke to the Jews, leading them to pick up stones to stone Him, as they recognized that His claim to preexistence was also a declaration of His divine authority. Refer to the following verses:

John 10:30-33

"I and the Father are one."
31 *Again His Jewish opponents picked up stones to stone Him.*
32 *But Jesus said to them, "I have shown you many good works from the Father. For which of these do you stone Me?"*
33 *"We are not stoning you for any good work," they replied, "but for blasphemy, because You, a mere man, claim to be God."*

Jesus' Authority as Revealed in John 1:1

A key element in John 1:1 is the explicit declaration of the authority Jesus held in heaven:

John 1:1

"...and the Word was God."

Here, the Apostle John unequivocally states the divine authority Jesus possessed in heaven, affirming that He was fully God.

This is the true authority of the Lord Jesus, as consistently affirmed in multiple passages throughout the Bible. We have already begun to explore this authority through the initial scriptures, and we will continue to examine it in detail in subsequent sections of this analysis.

Otherwise, in the scripture of John 1:1-3, I often hear a certain argument being constructed, which I would like to clarify and respond to briefly to dispel the confusion that some teachers attempt to introduce in order to diminish the fundamental meaning of this scripture and oppose its truth.

The argument presented here aims to challenge the explanation of this passage regarding the existence of the Word, who was with God and was God. To refute this clear explanation, some individuals use an example, claiming that accepting this passage in John is akin to saying: *"In the beginning, there was a stool, and the stool was with the carpenter, and the stool was the carpenter."*

This analogy, employed by some teachers within certain religious circles, often encourages their followers to vehemently oppose the truth of Jesus' divine authority.

The Fundamental Response to This Argument

If you carefully examine this argument, you will realize it is a weak one, particularly if you maintain intellectual calmness and first analyze the analogy being used. You will notice that the analogy conflates two distinct concepts that should not be compared. The concepts being conflated are the relationship between the Word and God and the relationship between a stool and a carpenter, without acknowledging that a stool is made of wood, while a carpenter is a person. Hence, these cannot reflect the unity and intrinsic relationship between the Word and God.

It is essential to understand that the relationship between the Word and God cannot be compared to that of a stool and a carpenter. Instead, it could be compared to the relationship between a stool and wood. In that sense, a more accurate analogy would be: *"In the beginning, there was a stool, and the stool was with the wood, and the stool was wood."*

This analogy aligns better with the passage in John, as it fundamentally relates to two interconnected concepts (stool and wood), thus reflecting the actual foundation and logic of the Gospel of John.

The Indivisibility of the Word and God

In summary, the analogy used by such teachers is flawed. In other words, it emphasizes that the Word and God are inherently inseparable authorities, just as you cannot separate a stool from wood, since the stool's essence is wood, just as Jesus' essence is divinity.

Analysis Question 4: If Jesus is God, why was He born and took on human flesh?

After addressing the many arguments and questions regarding the legitimacy of Jesus' divinity, this question naturally follows. The core issue here revolves around what appears to be a paradox: how can Jesus, who has a divine nature, also have a human form, a form He obtained through being born of Mary? This question often prompts further inquiries.

Why, if He is God, did He take on humanity?

The sin of Adam and Eve placed humanity in an immense debt that no human could repay. Let us read:

Genesis 3:17

"But you must not eat from the tree of the knowledge of good and evil, for when you eat from it, you will certainly die."

From this scripture, we read that when God placed Adam and Eve in the Garden of Eden, He gave them specific instructions about what they could and could not eat. They were forbidden from eating the fruit of the tree of the knowledge of good and evil. Alongside this prohibition,

God also warned them of the consequence of disobedience: death.

Clearly, God informed them of the danger they would face should they defy His command—they would surely die (*"for when you eat from it, you will certainly die"*). Hence, Adam and Eve's act of disobedience was equivalent to incurring a debt of sin, the penalty for which is death.

Romans 6:23

"For the wages of sin is death, but the gift of God is eternal life in Christ Jesus our Lord."

This is why Jesus, though divine, took on human form—to address the debt of sin that humanity could not repay. His incarnation was necessary for Him to serve as the perfect atoning sacrifice, bridging the gap between God and humanity.

And thus, humanity needed help to be rescued from this debt of sin. Therefore, it was necessary for an authority capable of addressing this debt to intervene to help humanity, as no human being has the ability to confront the debt of death. This is because death is beyond human capability, as David states:

Psalm 49:7-8 *"No one can redeem the life of another or give to God a ransom for them— the ransom for a life is costly, no payment is ever enough."*

This is a clear declaration from the Bible, showing that humans cannot save themselves or their neighbors, as the value of a human soul is beyond what any human can pay.

Given this, the fundamental question that arises is: what authority has the power to pay this debt of death and thus save humanity? To address this question, it is important to consider the key characteristics of the authority capable of performing this work. These characteristics must include:

1. **The ability to originate life (create).**
2. **Authority over death (mortality).**

Based on these attributes, it does not take long to identify who fulfills this role of redemption, given that these characteristics are evident in the Lord Jesus. The beauty of this is that all religious scriptures affirm this truth. Let us examine it further.

The Ability to Originate Life (Create)

From the perspective of the Bible, we already see in the Gospel of John that Jesus (the Word) is declared as the Creator of all things:

John 1:3 *"Through him all things were made; without him nothing was made that has been made."*

In other religious texts, the concept of Jesus' role in creation or His ability to originate life is acknowledged, although it is sometimes explained that Jesus was granted this ability by another authority. For instance, let us examine this in the **Quran**:

Quran 3:49 *"And He will make him a messenger to the Children of Israel, who will say, 'I have come to you with a sign from your Lord: I will create for you out of clay the form of a bird, then breathe into it, and it will become a bird by Allah's permission...'"*

This Quranic verse first acknowledges the fact that the Lord Jesus, during His ministry, performed an act of creating life by forming a bird from clay and breathing life into it, making the bird come alive. The Quran concludes by emphasizing that He performed this act "by the permission of Allah." However, this statement does not negate the involvement of the Lord Jesus in this act of creation, which is fundamentally an exclusive attribute of God.

If we set aside the debate on the context provided here, the central idea of the Lord Jesus being involved in creation remains the foundational element of this Quranic verse, highlighting His participation in this unique work of creation.

What further strengthens this argument is the uniqueness of the act of creation itself. God cannot share such a fundamental and sacred act with any ordinary being, as emphasized in the scriptures of both the Bible and other religious texts:

Isaiah 44:24 *"This is what the LORD says—your Redeemer, who formed you in the womb: I am the LORD, the Maker of all things, who stretches out the heavens, who spreads out the earth by myself."*

Here, God Himself underscores how sacred the act of creation is, stating that it is not an act He can delegate to any ordinary being, as the Creator is always superior to the created.

Moreover, to emphasize the importance of this point, the Quran also highlights that creation is one of the defining attributes that grants God the right to be worshiped by humanity for their fundamental needs:

Quran, Surah Al-Hajj 22:73 *"O people, an example is presented, so listen to it. Indeed, those you invoke besides Allah will never create [as much as] a fly..."*

In this context, we can agree that the mention of Jesus being involved in creation grants the Lord Jesus a rightful claim to divine authority.

Psalm 68:20 "Our God is a God who saves; from the Sovereign Lord comes escape from death."

Thus, according to the Bible, the responsibility of redeeming humanity is divine and pertains to God Himself. This underscores the idea of Jesus' coming for the purpose of redemption.

Jesus descended as a human from His divine nature to redeem us. I believe that based on these scriptural foundations, we have sufficient evidence showing how Jesus Christ is qualified for the task of redeeming humanity. The task of human redemption necessitates a person possessing two critical attributes: the ability to give life and to restore life that has been lost. To execute this task, it was necessary for Jesus to veil the glory of His divine authority and descend to redeem us. This act prompts the question of whether God can be born and appear in human form.

In addressing this question, it is essential to build a foundation by examining several scriptures from the Bible and then referencing other texts to deepen our understanding of this critical topic. Let us consider the following passages:

Exodus 33:20 "But," he said, "you cannot see my face, for no one may see me and live."

In this passage, God tells Moses that no human can see Him face to face and live. This statement introduces the challenge for God in His mission to redeem humanity: how can He approach humans in a way that does not destroy them but instead saves them?

This raises the fundamental question: **How can God reach humanity without causing their destruction from a direct encounter with His divine presence?** To answer this, let us look at the following verses:

Hebrews 2:16-17 "For surely it is not angels He helps, but Abraham's descendants. For this reason He had to be made like them, fully human in every way, in order that He might become a merciful and faithful high priest in service to God, and that He might make atonement for the sins of the people."

Here, the Bible provides an answer to the critical question, stating clearly that the nature God assumed to fulfill this mission was human. It also explains that, in carrying out this mission, Jesus needed to take on human form to accomplish the task of atoning for humanity's sins.

The Story of the Samaritan Woman

There was once a Samaritan woman living in a cold region. One day, as she warmed herself by the fire in her glass house, she saw a bird outside struggling in the cold. The bird, nearing death, found temporary relief by landing on a large tree outside a small window of the house.

Moved by compassion, the woman extended a long stick she used to stoke the fire, passing it through the small window to connect with the tree outside, creating a bridge for the bird to cross and enter her warm house. However, upon seeing the stick emerge from the window, the bird became frightened, mistaking it for a weapon meant to harm it. Terrified, the bird flew away into the freezing cold and ultimately died.

The Samaritan woman lamented, saying: "If only I had the ability to transform myself into a bird, I would have approached and reassured it, saying, 'Come inside with me to safety, my fellow bird!'"

This story emphasizes and sheds light on the importance of Jesus taking on human form in His efforts to reach and save humanity. Just as the Samaritan woman could not save the bird through her human methods, God needed to take on human form to effectively reach and redeem humankind.

If Jesus had come in the full splendor of His divine glory, humans would have been overwhelmed with fear and perished, as illustrated in the following biblical accounts...

Why Did Jesus Cry Out, "My God, My God, Why Have You Forsaken Me?"

In various theological discussions, this question has often been debated by religious teachers and scholars. The challenge arises from Jesus' statement on the cross in **Matthew 27:46**, where He cried out loudly:

"Eli, Eli, lema sabachthani?" (which means, "My God, my God, why have you forsaken me?")

This raises the question: Who was Jesus praying to, considering He is God?

The Core Answer to This Question

If Jesus' statement is taken at face value without deeper context, it might lead one to mistakenly think that Jesus was merely a human being. However, the foundation of biblical scripture connects this event to another dimension of Jesus' work—His assumption of humanity. Jesus deliberately took on human nature and placed Himself within human limitations to serve as an example and ultimately redeem humanity. This led Him, at times, to speak and act as a human being, despite His divine nature. The Apostle Paul clarifies this principle in his epistle:

Philippians 2:7-8 *"Rather, He made Himself nothing by taking the very nature of a servant, being made in human likeness. And being found in appearance as a man, He humbled Himself by becoming obedient to death—even death on a cross."*

The Bible explains that when Jesus assumed human form, He willingly set aside His glory. At times, He operated fully within the limitations of humanity rather than exercising His divine authority or power. Hence, His cry on the cross was made entirely from the perspective of His human experience. This, however, does not diminish His inherent divine authority, as it was part of the grand plan of redemption. By taking on humanity, He could "step into our shoes" and endure suffering on our behalf.

Jesus Was Fulfilling Prophecy

Another critical perspective is that Jesus' statement on the cross was also a fulfillment of prophecy. The Bible reveals this clearly when Jesus Himself said:

Luke 24:44 *"This is what I told you while I was still with you: Everything must be fulfilled that is written about Me in the Law of Moses, the Prophets, and the Psalms."*

This shows that Jesus' cry on the cross was intended to fulfill prophetic writings about Him, including those found in the Psalms of David. In **Psalm 22:1**, King David writes:

"My God, my God, why have you forsaken me?"

Jesus' statement on the cross mirrors this exact prophetic declaration. By doing so, He demonstrated that His mission aligned with the Scriptures, affirming His role in fulfilling what was written in the Law, the Prophets, and the Psalms.

Jesus Modeled Biblical Principles of Facing Trials Through Prayer and Song

In addition to fulfilling prophecy, Jesus' cry also exemplifies the biblical principle of handling trials through prayer and song. This principle is mentioned by the Apostle James:

James 5:13 *"Is anyone among you in trouble? Let them pray. Is anyone happy? Let them sing songs of praise."*

James outlines two heavenly principles for confronting adversity: prayer and the singing of psalms. Considering this, Jesus, in His humanity, faced the suffering of the cross by adhering to this principle. His statement on the cross was a direct quotation of **Psalm 22:1**, a psalm of David, thus fulfilling both the act of prayer and song. In this light, Jesus' action neither undermines nor negates His divine authority.

Conclusion

Jesus' cry, *"My God, My God, why have you forsaken me?"*, reflects His dual nature—fully human and fully divine. As a human, He bore the full weight of suffering and exemplified prayer and reliance on Scripture in the face of trials. At the same time, His actions fulfilled the prophetic words of Scripture, particularly those found in the Psalms.

This cry highlights the depth of His mission to redeem humanity without diminishing His eternal divinity.

Let us now move on to analyze another critical question regarding the divinity of Jesus.

Why Did He Sleep—Does God Sleep?

This fundamental question brings us to the conclusion of this analysis on the knowledge of the Trinity and the divinity of Jesus Christ. The question arises from the incident where Jesus was traveling with His disciples and was asleep on a cushion. When a severe storm struck, the disciples, in panic, woke Him to ask for help, as recorded in:

Mark 4:37-38 *"A furious squall came up, and the waves broke over the boat, so that it was nearly swamped. Jesus was in the stern, sleeping on a cushion. The disciples woke Him and said to Him, 'Teacher, don't you care if we drown?'"*

This act of Jesus sleeping, as narrated, sparks the question: if Jesus is God, how could He sleep? Supporters of this query often refer to the following scripture:

Psalm 121:4-5 *"Indeed, He who watches over Israel will neither slumber nor sleep."*

The Psalm states that God, as the guardian of Israel, neither slumbers nor sleeps. Thus, critics argue that Jesus' act of sleeping would deny His divinity.

The Core Answer to the Question

Essentially, this is one of the simpler questions concerning the Trinity and the divinity of Jesus Christ. The main issue lies in the failure to compare scriptures and examine multiple verses for context and reasoning. While **Psalm 121** is correct in stating that God does not sleep, the same Psalms also describe an instance where God appears as if He is asleep:

Psalm 78:65 *"Then the Lord awoke as from sleep, as a warrior wakes from the stupor of wine."*

In this verse, David describes the Lord awakening "as if from sleep," indicating a figurative sense rather than literal. The description conveys that the state of "slumber" here is not an actual loss of awareness or ability but an intentional pause or testing period.

With this explanation, we can align the situation of Jesus' sleep with the figurative sense used in Psalm 78:65. Jesus' sleep was not indicative of an inability but served a greater purpose of testing and teaching His disciples. This intentional "pause" aligns with the principle in **Isaiah 54:7**, where God momentarily leaves His people to test their faith:

Isaiah 54:7 *"For a brief moment I abandoned you, but with deep compassion, I will bring you back."*

Faith and Divine Authority

In this particular event, Jesus appeared to be asleep to test the faith of His disciples. Once He observed their faith turn toward Him during the storm, He immediately took action:

Mark 4:39-41 *"He got up, rebuked the wind, and said to the waves, 'Quiet! Be still!' Then the wind died down, and it was completely calm. He said to His disciples, 'Why are you so afraid? Do you still have no faith?' They were terrified and asked each other, 'Who is this? Even the wind and the waves obey Him!'"*

This event demonstrates the authority of Jesus over nature—a clear indicator of His divine power. Critics who focus solely on the act of sleeping miss the greater message conveyed in the narrative. The same Jesus who slept on a cushion is the One who commands storms to cease with mere words, affirming His divinity and mastery over creation.

Conclusion

The act of Jesus sleeping does not diminish His divinity. Instead, it reflects His dual nature as both fully God and fully human. His human nature allowed Him to experience fatigue and rest, while His divine nature enabled Him to still storms and exercise sovereignty over all creation. The story of Jesus calming the storm, rather than undermining His divinity, serves to affirm it in profound ways.

CHAPTER 03

IN WHAT FORM SHOULD GOD APPEAR FOR HUMANITY TO BE ABLE TO FACE HIM?

Should He come in the form of an ox? Or in the form of a lion? Or what form?

The Bible mentions how God revealed Himself in Christ in a way that humanity could confront and relate to.

1 Timothy 3:16

"Beyond all question, the mystery of godliness is great: He appeared in the flesh, was vindicated by the Spirit, was seen by angels, was preached among the nations, was believed on in the world, was taken up in glory."

The scriptures emphasize the method God used to reveal Himself to humanity—by taking on human form. Although His righteousness was recognized in the spiritual realm, He appeared in human flesh to make Himself relatable to humankind.

Can God appear in different forms?

Before concluding this aspect, it is worth exploring perspectives from other religious texts to enhance our understanding and perhaps open the minds of non-Christian readers.

Qur'an 57:3

"He is the First and the Last, the Apparent and the Hidden, and He is the All-Knowing of everything."

This verse highlights God's attributes, particularly His being both Apparent and Hidden. These attributes affirm the comprehensive ways in which God operates—both invisibly (Hidden) and visibly (Apparent). Interestingly, the Qur'an itself provides examples of both these modes of God's manifestations. One such example of His apparent presence is found in the story of Moses:

Qur'an 20:9-12

"Has the story of Moses reached you? When he saw a fire and said to his family, 'Stay here; indeed, I have perceived a fire. Perhaps I can bring you a torch or find guidance at the fire.' And when he came to it, he was called, 'O Moses! Indeed, I am your Lord, so remove your sandals. Indeed, you are in the sacred valley of Tuwa.'"

In this narrative, we see God revealing Himself to Moses through a burning bush. At first, Moses perceived it as an ordinary bush on fire, unaware that it carried the presence of God. Only when God declared, "Indeed, I am your Lord," did Moses recognize this divine encounter.

Was God born when He came as a human being?

In essence, God, as God, is neither born nor was He ever born. What is referred to as being "born of Mary" pertains solely to Jesus' humanity, which veiled His divinity. Mary did not give birth to God Himself but to the human nature that carried His divine essence. To suggest that Mary gave birth to divinity would imply that God had a beginning—that His existence started at birth—which contradicts the scriptural testimony:

Psalm 102:24-27

"I said: Do not take me away, my God, in the midst of my days; your years go on through all generations. In the beginning you laid the foundations of the earth, and the heavens are the work of your hands. They will perish, but you remain; they will all wear out like a garment. Like clothing you will change them, and they will be discarded. But you remain the same, and your years will never end."

Jesus' Own Testimony

To solidify this understanding, we can refer to Jesus' own words in His dialogue with the Jews. When they contested Jesus' claim of a relationship with Abraham, they pointed to His human birth through Mary and questioned His assertions based on His age. Let us read His response:

John 8:55-58

"'Your father Abraham rejoiced at the thought of seeing my day; he saw it and was glad.' They replied, 'You are not yet fifty years old, and you have seen Abraham?' 'Very truly I tell you,' Jesus answered, 'before Abraham was born, I am!'"

This profound statement underscores Jesus' preexistence and eternal nature, affirming that while His humanity had a beginning, His divinity has always existed.

Examples of God's Possibility to Take on Humanity

It is astonishing to witness opposition to this truth, despite the existence of various narratives that could serve as vital illustrations to simplify understanding of this matter. Consider the following story commonly shared in Dar es Salaam:

A young man was walking along a road when he met a beautiful woman whom he instantly liked. After some conversation, the woman agreed to visit his home. Upon arriving and sitting in the living room, the man asked her to pass him the TV remote control, which was a short distance from her. Shockingly, instead of standing up to retrieve it, the woman's arm stretched unnaturally far to grab the remote. This terrifying act caused the man to flee in panic, running out of the house and collapsing unconscious at the door.

Many recounting this story firmly believe that the woman was a demon disguised as a human being. What surprises me is how people readily accept that Satan can disguise himself to harm humans but strongly resist the idea that God can take on humanity to redeem us. Reflect deeply and change your perspective.

Jesus Took on Humanity to Reach Mankind

The Lord Jesus took on humanity to approach mankind and ultimately save them. The apostle John declared:

"The Word became flesh and dwelt among us, and we have seen His glory, glory as of the only Son from the Father, full of grace and truth." (John 1:14)

Therefore, the purpose of Jesus becoming flesh and dwelling among us should be received with gratitude, for it brought glory to humanity—unlike the harmful events associated with evil creatures that many tend to glorify. This act of Jesus living among us (after taking on human flesh) is described in Greek as:

Eskenosen — meaning "to pitch a tent" or "dwell among us."

Corroboration from Other Religious Texts

Beyond the Bible, I was delighted to find significant examples in other highly regarded religious texts, particularly the Qur'an, which illustrate the transformative ability to take on different forms for a specific purpose. For example, the Qur'an recounts the story of the angel who appeared to Mary in human form to avoid frightening her. Let us read from the scriptures:

"She placed a screen (to seclude herself) from them; then We sent to her Our Angel, and he appeared before her as a well-proportioned man." (Qur'an 19:17)

As previously stated, this is the story of Angel Gabriel, who appeared to Mary in a human form as narrated and believed by our Muslim brothers and sisters. The thought-provoking question here is: if an angel could transform into a human form, how could God not?

The Purpose of Jesus' Humanity

The truth is that the Lord Jesus took on that human form to conceal His glory, which mankind could not endure. Paul's epistle to the Corinthians summarizes this point:

"All this is from God, who reconciled us to Himself through Christ and gave us the ministry of reconciliation: that God was reconciling the world to Himself in Christ, not counting people's sins against them. And He has committed to us the message of reconciliation." (2 Corinthians 5:18-19)

Thus, it should be understood that Jesus' human form carried the full authority of divinity, an authority that existed eternally, even before Jesus' humanity was born through Mary.

If Jesus Is God, Why Did He Say He Was Going to His Father?

This question is among the significant debates in religious circles. The issue raised is that Jesus often referred to the Father in His conversations, leading some to question how Jesus could be God if He said He was going to His Father. What is the relationship between Jesus and the Father?

The Fundamental Answer

As previously elaborated, this relationship must be understood within the context of Jesus' mission and His dual nature—fully human and fully divine.

CHAPTER 04

THE PERSON OF THE HOLY SPIRIT

The Holy Spirit is not an inanimate force like many cults teach, but a being with intelligence, emotion, and will. The Holy Spirit is not an "it" but a "He". He is a Person. John 16: 12-14 [12] I have yet many things to say unto you, but ye cannot bear them now. [13] Howbeit when He, the Spirit of truth, is come, He will guide you into all truth: for He shall not speak of Himself; but whatsoever He shall hear, that shall He speak: and He will shew your things to come. [14] He shall glorify me: for He shall receive of mine and shall shew it unto you.

Who is a Person?

A person is an individual with a unique combination of physical, mental, and emotional characteristics. A person is capable of thinking, feeling, and communicating with others, and is often defined by their experiences, beliefs, and values. In legal terms, a person is an entity that has legal rights and responsibilities and is recognized by law as a distinct individual. In general, a person is a complex and multifaceted being that plays an important role in society and the lives of those around them.

Because the Holy Spirit's role is to point us towards Christ instead of Himself, many people misunderstand who the Holy Spirit is. Cults, for example, present Him as merely a force or power and as a result deny the Trinity. Christians must understand who the Holy Spirit is and be able to see from Scripture why we believe what we do about Him. So, we are going to take some time and, from the Bible, establish one point:

The Holy Spirit Is a Person

While this won't be an exhaustive list of proof texts it will be enough to give you a flavor of what the Bible teaches.

Holy Spirit is the Person, has intellect, will, emotions, and thinks for Himself, inter-alia, He is not controlled by God the Father or God the Son. He has His personality and He is God. The Holy Spirit has His mind, The Bible says that in [1 Corinthians 2: 10-11[10] these are the things God has revealed to us by His Spirit. The Spirit searches all things, even the deep things of God. [11] For who knows a person's thoughts except their spirit within them? In the same way, no one knows the thoughts of God except the Spirit of God].

1 Corinthians 2:10-11 is one of the verses that can be used as evidence that the Holy Spirit possesses His mind and thinks for Himself. This passage affirms that the Holy Spirit is capable of searching the deep things of God and revealing them to believers. This implies that the Holy Spirit is not merely a force or energy, but a divine person with the ability to think, reason, and communicate.

The Holy Spirit possesses personal characters

A. He has a mind...
1. "the mind of the Spirit" - Romans 8:27
2. This suggests thinking on His own

In the Bible, the Holy Spirit is referred to as a person rather than an impersonal force and is described as having a mind, will, and emotions. Romans 8:27, states that the Holy Spirit intercedes for believers with groanings that cannot be expressed in words and that he who searches hearts knows what is the mind of the Spirit. This suggests that the Holy Spirit has a mind and can think and communicate.

Furthermore, throughout the New Testament, the Holy Spirit is described as having the ability to teach, guide, and give understanding to believers (John 14:26, 1 Corinthians 2:10-13). These descriptions imply a level of intelligence and thinking on the part of the Holy Spirit.

B. He knows...
1. He "knows the things of God" - 1 Corinthians 2:11
2. Just as the "spirit of man" (a personal being) knows certain things

According to 1 Corinthians 2:11, the Holy Spirit "knows the things of God." This verse implies that the Holy Spirit has knowledge that is beyond human understanding, as it pertains to the mysteries of God. Additionally, the Holy Spirit is often described as a personal being within the Christian faith, distinct from both God the Father and Jesus Christ.

In terms of the analogy between the Holy Spirit and the "spirit of man," it is true that both are described as knowing. However, it's important to note that the knowledge of the Holy Spirit is not limited by human limitations or perspectives. Rather, the Holy Spirit is understood to have perfect knowledge and wisdom that comes directly from God.

C. He possesses affection...
1. Paul speaks of "the love of the Spirit" - Romans 15:30
2. When have you known of an "impersonal force" that could love?

In Romans 15:30, the apostle Paul speaks of "the love of the Spirit," which implies that the Holy Spirit is capable of love. This verse exhibits that the Holy Spirit is not just an impersonal force, but a personal being who is capable of expressing affection.

It is important to note that in Christian theology, the Holy Spirit is a distinct person within the Trinity, along with God the Father and Jesus Christ. As such, the Holy Spirit possesses all the attributes of a personal being, including the ability to love and be loved.

D. He has a will...
1. "The same Spirit works all these things, distributing to each one individually as He wills"
- 1 Corinthians 12:11
2. It was the Holy Spirit Who decided what person received which gift.

The Holy Spirit exhibits the attribute of a Person by displaying His will in 1 Corinthians 12:11 distributing gifts to "each one individually as He wills." In Acts 13:2, "As they ministered to the Lord and fasted, the Holy Spirit said, 'Now separate to Me Barnabas and Saul for the work to which I have called them.'" And again, in Acts 16:6 where Paul and Timothy, "were forbidden by the Holy Spirit to preach the word in Asia."

The Holy Spirit knows the very depth of God and it is His joy to reveal that to you only if you are clean enough to receive. [Romans 8:26-27 [26] In the same way, the Spirit helps us in our weakness. We do not know what we ought to pray for, but the Spirit himself intercedes for us through wordless groans. [27] And he who searches our hearts knows the mind of the Spirit because the Spirit intercedes for God's people by the will of God]. The Holy Spirit as a person is the only one capable of searching the depth of God and finding out God. Note that: God the Father, God the Son, and God, The Holy Spirit are separate but yet ONE.

For example, who knows you better than your spirit/yourself, nobody knows God but the Holy Spirit knows Him. Holy Spirit knows, and has the will of His own, for instance, He has His own separate will and has Intellect. And He shows emotion in Ephesians 4:30, "Do not grieve the Holy Spirit of God, by whom you were sealed for the day of redemption." Will, intelligence, and emotion are all attributes of a person.

The Holy Spirit is so different from the Father and the Son that He could have decided not to raise Jesus from the dead because He has His own WILL. He has His mind and makes His own decisions, yet He is faithful to Jesus and Jesus surrendered to the Holy Spirit before He became a "Man", (Jesus was conceived of the Holy Spirit in the womb of Mary - Mathews 1:20; Luke 1:30-35) simultaneously, knowing only the Holy Spirit could keep Him, empower Him, and raise Him from the Dead. If the Holy Spirit decided and or changed His mind about raising Jesus from the dead, you and I would not be saved and Jesus would have died and never rose from the dead.

When Jesus left heaven, He had no way to go back without the Holy Spirit. That tells us how much Jesus trusted the Holy Spirit. The Bible says, that when Jesus offered Himself to the Father, He offered Himself through the Holy Spirit. In other words, when the Father said to Jesus will you go, Jesus said I will go if the Holy Spirit will sustain me, empower me, and bring me back home, and the Holy Spirit said I will do it, Then Jesus said, I am completely surrendering to you. So, Jesus Christ surrendered to the Holy Spirit and gave Himself through the Holy Spirit.

The Holy Spirit was in full control of Jesus' life while on earth (Jesus was "filled with the Holy Spirit" - Luke 4:1); He anointed Him at the River Jordon, even sending Him to the wilderness to be tempted (He was "led by the Spirit" into the wilderness - Luke 4:1; Mathews 3:1) and performing miracle through Him.

Note: Those Miracles were performed through the power of the Holy Spirit, even Demons would not come out if the Holy Spirit was not there (Jesus claimed to cast out demons by the power of the Holy Spirit - Mathews 12:28). Jesus Himself said if I by the Spirit of God cast out devils, so, whose power, was it? By the Power of the Holy Spirit.

Now, If Jesus so needed the Holy Spirit, how about you? If, Jesus depended on Him, how about you and I? If Jesus trusted Him, why don't you trust the Holy Spirit? Holy Spirit is faithful; understand, how Faithful He has been to Jesus, He did not fail Him even ONE TIME. It is the Holy Spirit who decides what gift is given to the Body of Christ. God has given Him total responsibility for the Church. "But all these work that one and the self-same Spirit (refers to the fact that all the abilities and powers of the Gifts are produced and operated by the Spirit), dividing to every man severally as He (the Holy Spirit) will. (All the distribution is within the discretion of the Holy Spirit, which means that men or women cannot impart Gifts to other individuals. That is the domain of the Spirit Alone")

(1 Corinthians 12:11).

For God so loved the world that He gave His Only-begotten Son. Jesus came to the world and did the work of the Father, but it is the Holy Spirit that reveals the Word to the heart of men. It is the power of the Holy Spirit that manifests and reveals the work of Calvary. The Father said it, Jesus Did it, and The Holy Ghost revealed it.

Without the Holy Spirit, you will never know what happened. Where would you be, if the Holy Spirit did not reveal it? Christianity would not have survived a second after Jesus died. The Holy Spirit came to reveal, that He is the Great Revealer. Christianity is the Revelation. Christianity is not a religion, but it is the Revelation of Christ Jesus. Who is the Greater Revealer? The Holy Spirit! You would not have known Jesus without Him. You would have not known the Word of God there would be no Bible if the Holy Spirit had not revealed the Word of God to the Prophets.

The Holy Spirit has His own "will" and own "Emotions", just like you and I. The Bible said in Ephesians 4 Verse 29-30, [29] Do not let any unwholesome talk come out of your mouths, but only what helps build others up according to their needs, that it may benefit those who listen. [30] And do not grieve the Holy Spirit of God, with whom you were sealed for the day of redemption. That is what grieved him, the things people say.

The Holy Spirit is the only member of God's Head that gets grieved and wounded and He is extremely sensitive. People of God, you must understand that without the Holy Spirit, you can't do anything. The Holy Spirit is a Person, Intellect, Will, and Emotions.

The Holy Spirit suffers personal slights and injuries

A. He can be grieved ...
1. "Do not grieve the Holy Spirit of God" – Ephesians 4:30
2. He can be made sorrowful through our willful neglect

In Ephesians 4:30, the apostle Paul instructs believers not to "grieve the Holy Spirit of God." This suggests that the Holy Spirit is capable of experiencing emotions such as sorrow or disappointment, which can be caused by our actions or attitudes.

The teaching of grieving the Holy Spirit is also supported by other passages in the Bible. For example, in Isaiah 63:10, the prophet describes how the people of Israel "rebelled and grieved his Holy Spirit," leading to God's judgment. Similarly, in Psalm 78:40-41, the psalmist recounts how the Israelites "grieved him with their high places and moved him to jealousy with their idols."

The teaching of grieving the Holy Spirit affirms that the Holy Spirit is not simply an impersonal force or power, but a personal being with whom we can have a relationship. As such, our neglect or disobedience can have a real impact on the Holy Spirit and our relationship with Him.

B. He can be blasphemed ...
1. That is, to be spoken evil of
2. As in attributing His deeds to the works of Satan, the "unforgivable sin" - Matthews 12:31-32

Blaspheming the Holy Spirit can refer to both speaking evil of Him and also attributing His deeds to the works of Satan, which is referred to as the "unforgivable sin" in Matthew 12:31-32. This sin is considered unforgivable because it rejects the work of the Holy Spirit, who draws people to repentance and salvation in Jesus

Christ. Therefore, it is a serious offense against God that ultimately leads to a person's spiritual destruction.

C. He can be insulted …

1. One who has "trampled the Son of God underfoot" has also "insulted the Spirit of grace"

- Hebrews 10:29

2. This is done by sinning "willfully" - Hebrews 10:26

According to Hebrews 10:29, insulting the Spirit of grace is connected to the act of "trampling the Son of God underfoot." This passage indicates that one can insult the Holy Spirit by rejecting the work of Jesus Christ, who was sent by the Holy Spirit to bring salvation to humanity.

Furthermore, Hebrews 10:26 suggests that this insult to the Spirit of grace is committed by willful sinning, which is the deliberate rejection of God's commands and turning away from His will. This type of sin is particularly harmful because it hardens the heart and leads to a state of spiritual blindness, making it more difficult for a person to repent and turn back to God.

D. He can be lied to...

1. As Ananias and his wife Sapphira were guilty of doing

2. "...why has Satan filled your heart to lie to the Holy Spirit...?" - Acts 5:3

According to Acts 5:3, Ananias and his wife Sapphira lied to the Holy Spirit, which was considered a serious offense. This passage suggests that lying to the Holy Spirit is the same as lying to God, as the Holy Spirit is part of the triune Godhead.

Ananias and Sapphira were struck dead for their sin, which underscores the seriousness of this offense. This event serves as a warning to believers that lying to the Holy Spirit is a grave sin that carries significant consequences. Christians are called to be truthful and honest in their dealings with God and others and to seek forgiveness when they fall short of this standard.

E. He can be resisted ...

1. As Stephen charged the Jewish leaders of doing - Acts 7:51

2. This they did by resisting the message and persecuting the messengers who were inspired by the Holy Spirit - cf. Acts 7:52-53

The Bible says in Romans 15: [30] Now I beseech you, brethren, for the Lord Jesus Christ's sake, and the love of the Spirit, that ye strive together with me in your prayers to God for me; "For the Love of the Spirit", I heard many times people sing, Jesus Love Me this I know…., but I have ever heard The Holy Spirit Love me this I know…. Yes, The Holy Spirit loves you. 2 Corinthians 13: 14. An amazing prayer of the Holy Spirit is with you. Jesus walked in that fellowship, The Apostle and Saints walked in that fellowship…. If you want His Love and Grace, then never forget His communion, which means comradeship, participating with Him, and talking to Him this is the secret to power, victory, and freedom from sin. Where the Spirit of the Lord is there is Liberty. Liberty exists ONLY where the Holy Spirit is. So, if you want Liberty, look for where the Holy Spirit is.

Holy Spirit is the Power of the God Head, without Him, God the Father would not speak and would not act. He is Almighty God; He is the Power of God. Many people think the Holy Spirit is weaker than the Father and the Son because He is Third in the Trinity, the Holy Spirit is Third because of His work, He is the One who reveals, and He is the One who Manifest. Never forget He is the Power of the Trinity, He is the Power of the Father, He is the Power of God the Son. God Almighty Spoke the WORD, and God the Son became the WORD. God, the Holy Ghost, reveals the WORD. God the Father said Let us make man, it is Jesus (The Word) who squeezed the clay into the body, and it is the Holy Spirit who turned that mud/clay into Flesh and blood. If the Holy Spirit can turn mud into flesh, what can't He do to you?

The Holy Spirit is the One who took God (The Word) and made Him Man (Jesus). St. Matthew called Him the Child of the Holy Ghost. The Holy Ghost is The Power of the Mighty God. Note: It is not by might nor by power but by my Spirit says the LORD. Who do you think is in your Heart? It is the Spirit of Jesus called the Holy Ghost. John 14:26 Holy Spirit will teach you all things. The Bible says, if we don't have the Spirit of God, we are not His children.

When God the Father finished His work in the Old Testament, He left and never came back. When God the Father left, He sent the Son. The Son came to earth and did His work. When the Son left, He never came back, but He is coming back one day.

When the Son left, The Holy Ghost came and gave birth to the Church of Jesus Christ, revealed Jesus to the Church, and made Jesus real to His Church. Holy Spirit is Still HERE. Holy Spirit is still doing His work, one day His work will be over and He will leave; and when He leaves, we will go with HIM. When the Holy Spirit leaves, the Anti-Christ will come, The False Messiah will come and the Judgment will come upon the earth.

Remember, the Church hasn't seen The Father or Jesus nor heard the voice of the Father or the Son, but we have heard the voice of the Spirit, but wait a minute, you mean Jesus hasn't spoken to me, not once, the one you have been listening to all your life is the Holy Ghost, and you have called Him Jesus, you have called Him the Lord, you are correct, He is the Lord, HE IS THE SPIRIT OF THE LORD.

The Holy Ghost is Equal in Power, Majesty, and Glory. Now, the Holy Spirit will bring all things Jesus teaches into your remembrance. John 14: 26 He is the one who reminds you and teaches you! He testifies of Jesus. You see, at all times The Holy Spirit doesn't speak about Himself, ONLY Jesus.

The Holy Spirit is so powerful that He can convict the world of Sin. He convicts the world in John 16:8, "And when He has come, He will convict the world of sin, and of righteousness, and judgment." He performs miracles in Acts 8:39, "Now when they came up out of the water, the Spirit of the Lord caught Philip away so that the eunuch saw him no more; and he went on his way rejoicing."

He helps us by interceding on our behalf in Romans 8:26 "Likewise the Spirit also helps in our weaknesses. For we do not know what we should pray for as we ought, but the Spirit Himself makes intercession for us with groaning which cannot be uttered."

Convicting, interceding and teaching are all actions of a person.

Think about His Power, that He can convict the whole WORLD! Jesus said of Judgment too, the world will know that they will be judged because they have rejected the Messiah. The scripture says when the world/people see the Son of God in glory will wail and cry. That is what the Holy Ghost will do on that day. The Holy Spirit will show the world that God's Son is righteous. The Bible said the Holy Spirit will convince them of the judgment because they have rejected the Son of God. The Holy Spirit has so much Power that He will raise all of the Saints from the dead. It is the Holy Spirit Power that will transform your body in the twinkling of an eye. Holy Spirit is the Power of the Trinity.

In John 16:13 "However, when He, the Spirit of truth, has come, He will guide you into all truth". He guides you into all truth. A Person who guides and walks with you. A Person who guides takes you by the hand; A Person who guides is the one who is always with you. This awesome Person, The Holy Spirit is always with you, the Bible says so.

We have argued that the Holy Spirit is a person, and as such, is someone to whom human persons can relate directly. This is supported by the biblical descriptions of the personal ministry the Spirit performs in direct relationship to the individual believer. He is the one who convicts persons of sin, righteousness, and judgment (John 18-8-11); regenerates (John 3:5-80; guides into truth (John 16:513); sanctifies (Romans 8:1-17); and empowers for service (Acts 1:8). He is the one who inspires the writers produced the Scriptures (2 Timothy 3:16; 2 Peter 1:21). In one of these instances is it said that the Spirit works in conjunction with the Father and the Son.

I. The prominence of the Spirit in the Bible.
A. His mention in the Old Testament ...

1. The Old Testament mentions the Holy Spirit 88 times

2. 23 books in the Old Testament refer to the Holy Spirit

3. Although the actual expression "Holy Spirit" is used only 3 times - e.g., Psalms 51:11

4. Other expressions referring to the Spirit are used (e.g., "the Spirit of God") - Genesis 1:2
B. His mention in the New Testament...

1. The New Testament mentions the Holy Spirit 264 times

2. 60 or more references in the gospels

3. Acts has 57 references (which is why some call it "The Acts of The Holy Spirit")

4. The epistles refer to the Holy Spirit 132 times

5. Only 3 epistles make no mention of the Spirit (Philemon, 2 and 3 John)

Holy Spirit Personal actions. Holy Spirit speaks: Exhibit: "The Spirit speaks explicitly" (1 Timothy 4:1); "he that bath an ear, let him hear what the Spirit saith unto the churches" (Revelations 2:7). He teaches: "The Holy Spirit shall teach you in the same hour what ye ought to say" (Luke 12:12); "He shall teach you all things" (John 14:26). He commands or exercises authority: a striking proof of this is found in Acts 13:2, "The Holy Spirit said, separate unto me Barnabas and Saul for the work whereunto I have called them"—how utterly misleading would such language be if the Spirit were not a real person! He intercedes: "The Spirit itself maketh intercession for us" (Romans 8:26)— As the intercession of Christ proves Him to be a person, and a distinct one from the Father, unto whom He intercedes, so the intercession of the Spirit equally proves His personality, even His distinct personality.

CHAPTER 05

THE DEITY OF THE HOLY SPIRIT

The Holy Spirit is a Divine Being

The Holy Spirit is a divine being and a member of the Holy Trinity, which includes God the Father and Jesus Christ the Son. The Holy Spirit is the third person of the Trinity and is co-equal and co-eternal with God the Father and God the Son.

The Holy Spirit is the divine presence of God in the world and the hearts of believers. The Holy Spirit empowers Christians to live a godly life, helps them to understand the Bible, and guides them in their spiritual growth.

The Holy Spirit is the third person of the Holy Trinity along with God the Father and Jesus Christ the Son. This is based on the doctrine of the Trinity, which impeccably states that God is one divine being who exists in three distinct persons: the Father, the Son, and the Holy Spirit.

The Bible refers to the Holy Spirit using divine titles and attributes such as "the Spirit of God" (Genesis 1:2), "the Spirit of the Lord" (Isaiah 61:1), and "the Spirit of Truth"

(John 16:13). Additionally, in Acts 5:3-4, Ananias and Sapphira are said to have lied to the Holy Spirit and, in doing so, they are said to have lied to God.

Hence, the Holy Spirit is an essential part of the Christian doctrine of the Trinity and is a divine being who is co-equal and co-eternal with God the Father and God the Son.

A. His "Attributes" reveal His Divine nature ...

1. He is "Omniscient" (knows all things) - 1 Corinthians 2:10-11

2. He is "Omnipresent" (everywhere) - Psalms 139:7-10

3. He is called the "eternal" Spirit - Hebrews 9:14

B. His "Works" reveal His Divine nature...

1. He was involved in the "creation" of the world - Genesis 1:2; cf. also Job 33:4

2. He was involved in the "working of miracles" - Mathews 12:28; Ro 15:19

3. He was involved in the "redemption" of man - Hebrews 9:14

4. He is involved in the "regeneration" of man - John 3:5; Titus 3:4-6

All these supports the teaching of the Holy Spirit as the deity. Peter spoke of the Holy Spirit and God interchangeably in Acts 5:3-4,9. This makes sense only if the Holy Spirit is indeed God! But if the Holy Spirit is a personal, divine being...

- Does that mean the Bible teaches a polytheistic concept of God?

- Are there three Gods, or only one God?

- What relationship does the Holy Spirit maintain with the Father and with Jesus Christ?

Is the Holy Spirit a Deity or Not a Deity?

Having shown, then, that God's Infallible Word expressly and unequivocally teaches that the Holy Spirit is a Person, the following question to be considered is, under what character are we to consider Him? What rank does He occupy in the scale of self-existence?

It has been truly said that "He is either God, possessing, in a distinction of Person, an ineffable unity of the Divine nature with the Father and the Son, or He is the creature of God, infinitely removed from Him in essence and dignity, and having no other than a derivative excellence in that rank to which He is appointed in creation.

There is no medium between the one and the other. Nothing intermediate between the Creator and the created can be admissible. So that was the Holy Spirit to be placed at the top of all creation, even as high above the highest angel as that angel transcends the lowest reptile of animated life, the chasm would be still infinite; and He, who is emphatically called the Eternal Spirit, would not be God".

I will now attempt to exhibit from the Infallible Word that the Holy Spirit is distinguished by such names and attributes, that He is endowed with such a plentitude of underived power, and that He is the Author of such works as to altogether transcend finite ability, and such as can belong to none but God Himself.

However mysterious and inexplicable to human reason the existence of a distinction of Persons in the essence of the Godhead may be, yet if we submissively bow to the plain teachings of the Divine Oracles, then the conclusion that there subsists three Divine Persons who are co-essential, co-eternal, and co-equal is unavoidable. He of whom such works as the creation of the universe, the inspiration of the Scriptures, the formation of the humanity of Christ, the regeneration and sanctification of the elect, is, and must be GOD; or, to use the language of 2 Corinthians 3:17 "Now the Lord is that Spirit."

Biblical Evidence of the Deity of the Holy Spirit

1. Lying to the Holy Spirit is lying to God. To Ananias: Peter said, "Why hath Satan filled thine heart to lie to the Holy Spirit?" and then in the very next verse, he affirms "Thou hast not lied unto men, but unto God" (Acts 5:3, 4): if, then, lying to the Holy Spirit is lying to God, it necessarily follows that the Spirit must be God. Again, the saints are called "the temple of God," and the reason proving this is that, "the Spirit of God dwelleth in you" (1 Corinthians 3:16). In like manner, the body of the individual saint is designated, "the temple of the Holy Spirit," and then the exhortation is made, "therefore glorify God in your body" (1 Corinthians 6:19, 20). In 1 Corinthians 12, where the diversity of His gifts, administrations, and operations are mentioned, He is spoken of severally as "the same Spirit" (v. 4), "the same Lord" (v. 5), "the same God" (v. 6). In 2 Corinthians 6:16 the Holy Spirit is called "the living God."

2. The Holy Spirit is impeccably called Jehovah. The name that is utterly incommunicable to all creatures, and which can be applied to none except the Great Supreme. It was Jehovah who spoke by the mouth of all the holy Prophets from the beginning of the world (Luke 1:68, 70), yet in 2 Peter 1:20 it is implicitly declared that those Prophets all spoke by "the Holy Spirit" (see also 2 Samuel 23:2, 3, and compare Acts 1:16)! It was Jehovah whom Israel tempted in the wilderness, "sinning against God and

provoking the Most High" (Psalm 78:17, 18), yet in Isaiah 63:10 this is specifically termed, "rebelling against and vexing the Holy Spirit"! In Deuteronomy 32:12 we read, "The Lord alone did lead them," yet speaking of the same people, at the same time, Isaiah 63:14 declares, "The Spirit of the Lord did lead them." It was Jehovah who bade Isaiah, "Go and tell these people, hear ye indeed" (6:8, 9), while the Apostle declared, "Well spake the Holy Spirit by Isaiah the Prophet, saying, go unto the people and say, Hear ye indeed..." (Acts 28:25, 26)! What could more plainly establish the identity of Jehovah and the Holy Spirit? Note that the Holy Spirit is called "the Lord" in 2 Thessalonians 3:5.

3. The flawlessness and veracity of God are all found in the Spirit. By what is the nature of any being determined but by its properties? He who possesses the properties peculiar to an angel or man is rightly esteemed one. So, He who possesses the attributes or properties which belong alone to God must be considered and worshipped as God.

The Scriptures very clearly and abundantly affirm that the Holy Spirit is possessed of the attributes peculiar to God. They ascribe to Him absolute holiness. As God is called "Holy," "the Holy One," being therein described by that superlatively excellent property of His nature wherein He is "glorious in holiness" (Exodus 15:1 1); so is the Third Person of the Trinity designated "the Spirit of Holiness" (Romans 1:4) to denote the holiness of His nature and the Deity of His Person. The Spirit is eternal (Hebrews 9:14). He is omnipresent: "Whither shall I flee from thy Spirit?" (Psalms 139:7). He is omniscient (see 1 Corinthians 2:10, 11). He is omnipotent: being termed "the Power of the Highest" (Luke 1:35; see also Micah 2:8, and compare

Isaiah 40:28).

4. The Holy Spirit omnipotently manifested the Trinity. As exhibited in Matthew 4:1 we are told, "Then was Jesus led up of the Spirit into the wilderness": Who but a Divine Person had the right to guide and or instruct the Mediator? And to whom but God would the Redeemer have submitted! In John 3:8 the Lord Jesus drew an analogy between the wind which "bloweth where it listeth" (not being at the disposal or direction of any creature), and the imperial operations of the Spirit.

In 1 Corinthians 12:11, it is expressly affirmed that the Holy Spirit has the distribution of all spiritual gifts, having nothing but His pleasure for His rule. He must, then, be "God over all, blessed forever." In Acts 13:2-4 we find the Holy Spirit calling men unto the work of the ministry, which is solely a Divine prerogative, though wicked men have abrogated it unto themselves. In these verses, it will be found that the Spirit appointed their work, commanded them to be set apart by the church, and sent them forth. In Acts 20:28 it is declared that the Holy Spirit set officers over the church.

5. The works ascribed to the Spirit demonstrate His Godhead. Holy Spirit is involved in the creation and is attributed to Him, no less than to the Father and the Son: "By the Spirit, lie hath garnished the heavens" (Job 26: 13): "The Spirit of God hath made me" (Job 33:4). He is concerned in the work of providence (Isaiah 40:13-15; Acts 16:6, 7). All Scripture is given by inspiration of God (2 Timothy 3:16), the source of which is the Spirit Himself (2 Peter 1:21). The humanity of Christ was miraculously formed by the Spirit (Matthew 1:20). Christ was anointed for His work by the Spirit (Isaiah 61:1; John 3:34). His miracles were performed by the Spirit's power (Matthew

12:3 8). He was raised from the dead by the Spirit (Romans 8:11). Who but a Divine person could have wrought such works as these!?

Reader, do you have personal and inward proof that the Holy Spirit is none other than God? Has He wrought in you that which no finite power could? Has He brought you from death unto life, made you a new creature in Christ, imparted to you a living faith, and filled you with holy longings after God? Does He breathe into you the spirit of prayer, take of the things of Christ and show them unto you, apply to your heart both the precepts and promises of God? If so, then, these are so many witnesses in your bosom of the deity of the Blessed Spirit.

ABSTRACT:

He is called God

Acts 5:3-4 But Peter said, Ananias, why hath Satan filled thine heart to lie to the Holy Ghost, and to keep back part of the price of the land? 4. Whiles it remained, was it not thine own? and after it was sold, was it not in theirpower? why hast thou conceived this thing in thine heart? thou hast not lied untomen, but unto God.

(Compare: Exodus 17:7 - Psalms 95:6-11 - Hebrews 3:7-11)

Exodus 17:7 And he called the name of the place Massah, and Meribah, because of the chiding of the children of Israel, and because they tempted the Lord, saying, Is the Lord among us, or not?

Psalms 95:6-11 O come, let us worship and bow down: let us kneel before the Lord our maker. For He is our God, and we are the people of his pasture, and the sheep of his hand. Today if ye will hear his voice, Harden not your heart, as in the provocation, and as in the day of temptation in the wilderness: When your fathers tempted me, proved me, and saw my work. Forty years long was I grieved with this generation, and said, it is a people that do errin their heart, and they have not known my ways: Unto whom I swear in my wrath that they should not enter into my rest.

Hebrews 3:7-11 Wherefore (as the Holy Ghost saith, today if ye will hear his voice, Harden not your hearts, as in the provocation, in the day of temptation in the wilderness: When your fathers tempted me, proved me, and saw my works forty years. Therefore, I was grieved with that generation, and said, they do always err in their heart, and they have not known my ways. So, I swear in my wrath, they shall not enter into my rest.)

A. He is Omnipresent

Psalms 139:7 Whither shall I go from thy Spirit? or whither shall I flee from thypresence?

1 Corinthians 12:13 For by one Spirit are we all baptized into one body, whether we be Jews or Gentiles, whether we be bond or free; and have been all made to drink into one Spirit.

The veracity that the Holy Spirit is omnipresent is a core doctrine in Christianity. According to Psalm 139:7, the Holy Spirit is not limited by space or time and is present everywhere at all times.

This truth is based on several biblical passages that describe the Holy Spirit's presence and work in the world. For example, Psalm 139:7-8, it says, "Where can I go from your Spirit? Where can I flee from your presence? If I go up to the heavens, you are there; if I make my bed in the depths, you are there."

Similarly, in John 14:16-17, Jesus promised His disciples that He would ask the Father to send them the

Holy Spirit, who would be with them forever: "And I will ask the Father, and he will give you another advocate to help you and be with you forever—the Spirit of truth."

The belief in the omnipresence of the Holy Spirit is significant for Christians because it means that God's presence is not limited to a particular place or time. The Holy Spirit is always with believers, guiding and empowering them in their spiritual lives.

A. He is Omniscient

The Holy Spirit is omniscient, meaning that the Spirit is all-knowing. This truth is based on several passages in the Bible that describe the Spirit's knowledge and understanding.

For example, 1 Corinthians 2:10-11 states, "These are the things God has revealed to us by his Spirit. The Spirit searches all things, even the deep things of God. For who knows a person's thoughts except the spirit within them? In the same way, no one knows the thoughts of God except the Spirit of God." This passage suggests that the Holy Spirit has a deep knowledge of God and can reveal that knowledge to believers.

Similarly, John 14:26 states, "But the Advocate, the Holy Spirit, whom the Father will send in my name, will teach you all things and will remind you of everything I have said to you." This passage suggests that the Holy Spirit can teach and remind believers of important truths.

Overall, the fact that the Holy Spirit's omniscience is based on the above-exhibited verses that the Spirit is all-knowing, a divine being, and part of the Holy Trinity (along with God the Father and Jesus Christ). As such, the Spirit has the same attributes as God, including omniscience.

A. He is Omnipotent

Luke 1:35-37 And the angel answered and said

unto her, The Holy Ghost shall comeupon thee, and the power of the Highest shall overshadow thee: therefore, also that holything which shall be born of thee shall be called the Son of God.

36. And, behold, thy cousin Elisabeth, she hath also conceived a son in her old age: andthis is the sixth month with her, who was called barren.

37. For with God nothing shall be impossible.

Romans 8:11 But if the Spirit of him that raised Jesus from the dead dwell in you, He that raised Christ from the dead shall also quicken your mortal bodies by his Spirit that dwelleth in you.

The Holy Spirit possesses the attributes of omnipotence, such as the ability to perform miraculous acts and to bring about spiritual transformation in individuals and communities. Others may interpret the term "omnipotence" differently or may have different theological beliefs altogether.

A. His part in Creation

The Holy Spirit has played a role in the creation of the universe, alongside God the Father and Jesus Christ the Son. This truth is based on several passages in the Bible, including the opening verses of the Book of Genesis, which describe the Spirit of God as hovering over the waters at the time of creation:

"In the beginning, God created the heavens and the earth. Now the earth was formless and empty, darkness was over the surface of the deep, and the Spirit of God was hovering over the waters." (Genesis 1:1-2)

This passage advocates that the Holy Spirit was present at the time of creation and may have played a role in bringing order to the creation. Additionally, in the Gospel of John, the Holy Spirit is described as the one who gives life and sustains all things:

"In the beginning was the Word, and the Word was with God, and the Word was God. He was with God in the beginning. Through him all things were made; without him, nothing was made that has been made... In him was life, and that life was the light of all mankind." (John 1:1-4)

Psalms 104:30 Thou sendest forth thy spirit, they are created: and thou renewest theface of the earth.

Job 26:13 By his spirit, he has garnished the heavens; his hand has formed the crooked serpent.

B. Works Miracles

Matthew 12:28 reads: "But if it is by the Spirit of God that I cast out demons, then the kingdom of God has come upon you." This statement was made by Jesus in response to accusations from the Pharisees that he was casting out demons by the power of Beelzebub, the prince of demons.

In this passage, Jesus affirms that his ability to cast out demons is due to the power of the Holy Spirit, who is often referred to as the Spirit of God in the Bible. By attributing his power to the Spirit of God, Jesus is emphasizing the divine origin and nature of his ministry. He is also indicating that his work is part of God's plan to establish his kingdom on earth.

The concept of the kingdom of God is a central theme in Jesus' teaching. It refers to the rule and reign of God over all things, including the hearts and lives of people. Jesus is saying that by casting out demons through the power of the Holy Spirit, he is demonstrating the reality and presence of God's kingdom in the world. This was an important message for the people of his time, who were looking for a savior and longing for God's kingdom to be established on earth.

  C. Equal with the Father and Son

Matthew 3:16-17, which describes the baptism of Jesus by John the Baptist. The passage reads as follows:

"And Jesus, when he was baptized, went up straightway out of the water: and, lo, the heavens were opened unto him, and he saw the Spirit of God descending like a dove, and lighting upon him: And lo a voice from heaven, saying, This is my beloved Son, in whom I am well pleased."

This passage is significant because it marks the beginning of Jesus' public ministry. The baptism of Jesus is seen as a symbolic act of cleansing and a public declaration of his identity and mission.

In this passage, the Holy Spirit is depicted as descending on Jesus like a dove, which is a symbol of peace, gentleness, and purity. This image emphasizes the role of the Holy Spirit in Jesus' ministry, as the Spirit empowered Jesus to carry out his mission and perform miracles.

The voice from heaven, which is identified as the voice of God the Father, affirms Jesus' identity as the beloved Son of God and expresses God's pleasure and approval of him. This declaration emphasizes the divine nature of Jesus and his unique relationship with God the Father.

Overall, this passage highlights the important role of the Holy Spirit in Jesus' ministry and emphasizes Jesus' divine identity and mission as the Son of God.

Matthew 28:19-20 Go ye therefore, and teach all nations, baptizing them in thename of the Father, and of the Son, and the Holy Ghost: 20. Teaching them to observe all things whatsoever I have commanded you: and, lo, I am with you always, even unto the end of the world. Amen.

2 Corinthians 13:14 The grace of the Lord Jesus Christ, and the love of God, and the communion of the Holy Ghost, be with you all. Amen.

D. He is Eternal

Hebrews 9:14 How much more shall the blood of Christ, who through the eternal Spirit offered himself without spot to God, purge your conscience from dead works toserve the living God?

The Holy Spirit is one of the three persons of the Holy Trinity, alongside God the Father and Jesus Christ the Son. As such, the Holy Spirit is eternal, meaning that the Spirit has no beginning or end and has always existed.

This truth is rooted in several passages of the Bible, including in the Gospel of John, where Jesus speaks about the Holy Spirit as the "Spirit of Truth" who will abide with the disciples forever (John 14:16-17) and as the one who will guide them into all truth (John 16:13). Additionally, in the book of Acts, the Holy Spirit is described as descending upon the apostles on the day of Pentecost, indicating that the Spirit has a continuing presence in the world.

Accordingly, the eternal nature of the Holy Spirit is a fundamental aspect of Christian theology, reflecting the truth that God exists outside of time and space and is infinite and unchanging.

CHAPTER 06

COMPARISON BETWEEN THE BIBLE AND THE QURAN REGARDING THE CONCEPT OF THE TRINITY

The Holy Trinity According to The Bible

First of all, it should be understood that Almighty God is very exalted, and we, as His creatures, find it difficult to comprehend Him as we wish. God is omnipotent; we cannot limit Him by saying He can do this and that He cannot do that. We cannot fully comprehend God until He fits into our understanding; we cannot know His limits and boundaries. The day a human being can fully understand God, He will cease to be God.

What we can understand is how He has revealed Himself to us through His Holy Scriptures. It would be strange to start denying how God wants us to understand Him through His Word. Therefore, it is my intention to present the Scriptures as God wants us to understand Him.

The Bible teaches that God is One but in Three Eternal Personalities.

In the Book of Genesis 1:1-3, we read:
"In the beginning, God created the heavens and the earth. Now the earth was formless and empty, darkness was over the surface of the deep, and the Spirit of God was hovering over the waters."

We can say there is 1. God and 2. His Spirit. Then the scriptures continue to say:

"And God said, 'Let there be light,' and there was light" (Genesis 1:3).

So, we see that according to these scriptures, there is God, His Spirit, and His Word.

These are living Personalities, each independently functioning according to God's will.

There is ample evidence in the Scriptures showing that these Persons of God have been active throughout human history.

For example, in Genesis 6:3, we read:
"Then the LORD said, 'My Spirit will not contend with humans forever…'.'" So, the Spirit of God can contend.

Isaiah 44:3:
"…I will pour out my Spirit on your offspring…."

The Spirit of God, as a living Person, can be grieved or offended by humans.

Matthew 12:31:
"And so I tell you, every kind of sin and slander can be forgiven, but blasphemy against the Spirit will not be forgiven."

Ephesians 4:30:
"And do not grieve the Holy Spirit of God, with whom you were sealed for the day of redemption."

The Holy Spirit preached the gospel in the Old Testament through the prophets.

The prophets spoke the Word of God under the guidance of the Holy Spirit.

1 Peter 1:11:
"They were told that their messages were not for themselves, but for you. And now this Good News has been announced to you by those who preached in the power of the Holy Spirit sent from heaven…."

2 Peter 1:21:
"For prophecy never had its origin in the human will, but prophets, though human, spoke from God as they were carried along by the Holy Spirit."

In Romans 8:26, we see that:
"…the Spirit himself intercedes for us through wordless groans."

All these attributes of the Spirit tell us that the Holy Spirit of God is the living Person of God's operation. In other words, the Holy Spirit is God Himself.

Jesus Himself said:
"God is spirit, and his worshipers must worship in the Spirit and in truth" (John 4:24).

Who is the Word of God in the Bible?

The Holy Scriptures (the Bible) tell us that God created the heavens and the earth by His Word. When you read Genesis 1:4-31, you will find that God spoke the Word of creation, and it came into being. Psalm 33:6 says:
"By the word of the LORD the heavens were made, their starry host by the breath of his mouth."

When we carefully examine the scriptures, we discover that the Word of God is alive and powerful (read Hebrews 4:12) and has the power to give life. In this sense, we can conclude that, just as the Spirit of God is a living Personality, so is the Word of God.

As we saw, the act of creation was carried out by the Word of God, the second Person of the Godhead. Throughout the Bible, there is evidence of this cooperation between God, His Word, and His Spirit in creation. The Word Himself says in Proverbs 8:22-30 about His participation in the work of creation:

"The LORD brought me forth as the first of his works, before his deeds of old; I was formed long ages ago, at the very beginning, when the world came to be…then I was constantly at his side. I was filled with delight day after day, rejoicing always in his presence."

The Bible is very clear that this Word who created the heavens and the earth is also God. This is because you cannot separate God from His Word and say God is God and His Word is not God but something different. God and His Word are One. We read in John 1:1-3 that:

"In the beginning was the Word, and the Word was with God, and the Word was God…through him all things were made; without him nothing was made that has been made."

Throughout the Bible, we see the Word actively working and being given the attribute of a living Personality of God.

Now the time comes to fulfill another great work of redeeming fallen humanity. As always in God's work, the principal actor is "His Word." So, God sent His Word to complete the work of redemption.

The Word became flesh to accomplish human redemption.

God's principle regarding redemption is that:
"Without the shedding of blood, there is no forgiveness" (Hebrews 9:22).

Thus, we see that:
"…since the children have flesh and blood, he too shared in their humanity so that by his death he might break the power of him who holds the power of death—that is, the devil" (Hebrews 2:14).

Therefore, to redeem humanity:
"The Word became flesh and made his dwelling among us. We have seen his glory, the glory of the one and only Son, who came from the Father, full of grace and truth" (John 1:14).

This act of the Word agreeing to become flesh is what led to Him being called the "Son of God." As we saw in the above scripture, it is not in a physical sense as humans procreate. God Himself declared after the Word became flesh that:
"You are my Son; today I have become your Father." And again, "I will be his Father, and he will be my Son." (Hebrews 1:5).

"And a voice from heaven said, 'This is my Son, whom I love; with him I am well pleased'" (Matthew 3:17).

By the Word becoming flesh, we then have the title of God the Father, God the Son, and God the Holy Spirit. This is due to the fact that the act of the Word becoming flesh does not strip Him of His divinity. What we can see here is that the Word of God took on flesh, leading to a union of the Word (God) and flesh (Man). In Jesus, there is the fullness of God in His divinity and the fullness of humanity in His human body. The Word (Jesus) Himself says:
"...sacrifices and offerings you did not desire, but a body you prepared for me; with burnt offerings and sin offerings you were not pleased. Then I said, 'Here I am—it is written about me in the scroll—I have come to do your will, my God.'" (Hebrews 10:5-7).

We see that the Word was given a body, took on humanity, and we saw Him with all the attributes of humanity. But by His nature:

"…being in very nature God, did not consider equality with God something to be used to his own advantage; rather, he made himself nothing by taking the very nature of a servant, being made in human likeness." (Philippians 2:6-7).

In this union, He was born of a woman, and the angel told Mary, who was to bear the Son, that:

"You will conceive and give birth to a son, and you are to call him Jesus. He will be great and will be called the Son of the Most High (that is, God)…The Holy Spirit will come on you, and the power of the Most High will overshadow you. So, the holy one to be born will be called the Son of God." (Luke 1:31-32, 35).

Later, the angel Gabriel told Joseph, Mary's fiancé, the same words he told Mary:

"She will give birth to a son, and you are to give him the name Jesus, because he will save his people from their sins" (Matthew 1:21).

What confuses many is when the Word became flesh and appeared in the form of a human. In that form, Jesus had all the human needs, such as hunger, thirst, sleep, circumcision on the eighth day, tears, fatigue, etc., like any other human being.

We need to understand that Jesus came to show us how to live a victorious life against sin by relying on God as human beings. The scriptures testify that He was tempted as we are

tempted, yet without sin. He had no blemish throughout His life. The Holy Scriptures say:
"But we have one who has been tempted in every way, just as we are—yet he did not sin" (Hebrews 4:15).

"He committed no sin, and no deceit was found in his mouth" (1 Peter 2:22).

In His human state, He relied on God for everything. This is why you will see that He prayed to God the Father, and you will also see that He made statements like:
"...do not hold on to me, for I have not yet ascended to the Father

. Go instead to my brothers and tell them, 'I am ascending to my Father and your Father, to my God and your God'" (John 20:17).

In the state of divinity that was within Him (the Word of God), He said statements such as:
"I and the Father are one" (John 10:30).

"Anyone who has seen me has seen the Father" (John 14:9).

"Believe me when I say that I am in the Father and the Father is in me; or at least believe on the evidence of the works themselves" (John 14:11).

How was the Father in Jesus? By the Word that took on the human body; the Word of God was in the flesh, and the flesh was in the Word of God. That is Jesus.

In this state, it is not surprising to call Jesus God, and indeed, He is not only God but:
"...Christ Jesus, our great God and Savior" (Titus 2:13).

Thus, the concept of the Holy Trinity (one God in three Persons) is very evident within the Holy Scriptures, and there is no need for much argument, except to deny the scriptures. As I said earlier, we humans should not dictate to God how He should be and how He should not be. What we can do is to receive by faith how He has revealed Himself to us and what He has shown us. The scriptures say:
"The secret things belong to the LORD our God, but the things revealed belong to us and to our children forever..." (Deuteronomy 29:29).

Up to this point, we have seen in the Bible that God is One but has revealed Himself to us in three Persons of His operation. In the Old Testament, these Persons are God, His Word, and His Spirit, and in the New Testament, after the Word became flesh, these Persons take on the title of God the Father, God the Son, and God the Holy Spirit. Now let us turn to the Noble Quran and see if, 600 years later, God would change His revelations and teach otherwise.

The Holy Trinity According to The Noble Quran

Since in examining the Holy Trinity in the Bible, we started from the beginning during creation, we must follow the same approach for this subject.

The Holy Spirit according to the Noble Quran.

Just as in the Bible, the Noble Quran agrees that God created the heavens and the earth in six days.
"It is He who created the heavens and the earth in six days—and His Throne was upon the water—that He might test you as to which of you is best in deed. But if you were to say, 'You are indeed to be raised up after death,' those who disbelieve would surely say, 'This is not but obvious magic'" (Surah 11:7, HUD).

Abdalla Farsy, a Swahili commentator of the Quran, explains in his commentary on this verse:
"And saying that the heavens and the earth were created in six days, God knows Himself, what exactly those six days are according to His own calculation. And that Throne of God we do not know nor do we know about the WATER upon which the Throne was" (Abdalla Farsy, Tafsiri ya Quran Tukufu, Surah 11:7).

It appears that the interpreters of the Quran fail to understand these words about God's creation. But they should not struggle; what they need to do is follow the advice given within the Noble Quran itself. In Surah 10:94, we read:
"So if you are in doubt about what We have revealed to you, then ask those who have been reading the Scripture before you (the Jews and the Christians)" (Surah 10:94).

To understand those days of creation and how the Throne of God was upon the water at that time of creation, one needs to read the Bible as we saw earlier. The Bible states that the days consist of "evening and morning," making up

a day (read Genesis 1). Morning and evening can only occur within a 24-hour period. Thus, those six days are days of 24 hours each. The Bible also says:
"For in six days the LORD made the heavens and the earth, the sea, and all that is in them, but He rested on the seventh day. Therefore the LORD blessed the Sabbath day and made it holy" (Exodus 20:11).

*"*Thus the heavens and the earth were completed in all their vast array. By the seventh day God had finished the work he had been doing; so on the seventh day he rested from all his work" (Genesis 2:1-2).

The Quran also agrees with the Bible that God was upon the water during creation. According to the Bible, it was the Spirit of God that was hovering over the surface of the waters (Genesis 1:2).

Many verses in the Quran show that the Spirit of God is sent from God to strengthen His servants (Prophets), for example:
"He sends down the angels with the Spirit by His command upon whom He wills of His servants, (saying), 'Warn that there is no deity except Me; so fear Me'" (Surah 16:2, An-Nahl).

"Exalted above (all) degrees, (He is) the Possessor of the Throne. He places the Spirit of His command upon whom He wills of His servants to warn of the Day of Meeting" (Surah 40:15, Al-Mu'min).

Many Quranic commentators like Abdalla Farsy interpret the word "spirit" (rooh) used in these verses of the Quran to mean Revelation or Message or Prophethood that God gives to His prophets. This verse of Surah 40:15 in Abdalla Farsy's commentary reads:

"He is the Exalted in ranks, the Possessor of the Throne. He sends down the Revelation of His command upon whom He wills of His servants to warn of the Day of Meeting" (Abdalla Farsy, Tafsiri ya Quran Tukufu, Surah 40:15).

Here, the Arabic word "rooh" (spirit) is interpreted as "wahyi" (revelation). Perhaps to avoid the direct understanding that God sends His Holy Spirit to the prophets and messengers to give the warning messages. However, this still agrees with the concept we saw in the Bible that prophets delivered their messages under the guidance of the Holy Spirit.

"For prophecy never had its origin in the human will, but prophets, though human, spoke from God as they were carried along by the Holy Spirit" (2 Peter 1:21).

Jesus Himself, after becoming flesh (in His humanity), both the Bible and the Quran testify that He was strengthened by the power of the Holy Spirit to perform many miracles.
"And We gave Moses the Book and followed him up with a succession of messengers. And We gave Jesus, the son of Mary, clear proofs and supported him with the Holy Spirit. But is it (not) that every time a messenger came to you (Israelites) with what your souls did not desire, you were arrogant? And a party (of messengers) you denied and another party you killed" (Surah 2:87, Al-Baqara).

"When Allah will say, 'O Jesus, son of Mary, remember My favor upon you and upon your mother when I supported you with the Pure Spirit and you spoke to the people in the cradle and in maturity; and when I taught you writing and wisdom and the Torah and the Gospel; and when you designed from clay (what was) like the form of a bird with My permission, then you breathed into it, and it became a bird with My permission; and you healed the blind and the leper with My permission; and when you brought forth the dead with My permission; and when I restrained the Children of Israel from (killing) you when you came to them with clear proofs, and those who disbelieved among them said, 'This is nothing but obvious magic'" (Surah 5:110, Al-Ma'ida).

These words are also found in the Bible, that Jesus was empowered by the Holy Spirit. Jesus said:
"The Spirit of the Lord is on me, because he has anointed me to proclaim good news to the poor. He has sent me to proclaim freedom for the prisoners and recovery of sight for the blind, to set the oppressed free" (Luke 4:18).

The lack of detailed explanations about the Holy Spirit and His work in the Quran does not mean that there is no Person of God called the Holy Spirit. This absence might be because the Prophet Muhammad (PBUH) himself was revealed to:
"And they ask you, (O Muhammad), about the Spirit. Say, 'The Spirit is of the affair of my Lord. And mankind has not been given of knowledge except a little'" (Surah 17:85, Al-Israa).

According to this verse, Allah (SWT) says that Muhammad was given only a little knowledge about the matters concerning the Holy Spirit. However, even this little knowledge, when read in the light of the Holy Bible, we can see the consistent chain of teaching about the Holy Spirit.

After seeing the presence of the Holy Spirit from God within the Noble Quran, let us now look at the "Word of God" and His work within the Quran.

The Word from Almighty God according to the Noble Quran

In the Bible, we saw that the Word of God created the heavens and the earth. Is there any difference in the Quran? No, we read in Surah 2:117:
"The Originator of the heavens and the earth. When He decrees a matter, He only says to it, 'Be,' and it is" (Surah 2:117, Al-Baqara).

These words completely align with

 the words in the Holy Bible that:
"By the word of the LORD the heavens were made, their starry host by the breath of his mouth ... For he spoke, and it came to be; he commanded, and it stood firm" (Psalm 33:6,9).

Thus, we see that both the Bible and the Quran agree that the heavens and the earth were created by the Word of God. In the Bible, we saw that this Word became flesh and lived among us. Can we find evidence in the Quran that the Word became flesh?

The Word that became flesh according to the Noble Quran

In Surah 3:45, we read:
"(Remember) when the angels said, 'O Mary, indeed Allah gives you good tidings of a word from Him, whose name will be the Messiah, Jesus, the son of Mary, distinguished in this world and the Hereafter and among those brought near (to Allah)."

In this verse, we are told that Prophet Jesus (Isa) is a Word from God, and He has honor in this world and the Hereafter. As He Himself said in Matthew 28:19, "All authority in heaven and on earth has been given to me."

Throughout the Quran, Prophet Jesus (Isa) is described as the Word from God.

Why then do Muslims deny the divinity of Jesus or the Holy Trinity, despite the abundant evidence within the Quran?

To be truthful, there are no scriptures within the Quran that directly deny that Jesus or Prophet Isa is not God, or that reject the concept of the Holy Trinity, i.e., One God in three Persons (note that when the Quran says that God is One, it does not mean denying the Holy Trinity. The Bible also teaches that God is One, but this oneness is in three Persons as we saw in this study).

Many explanations within the Quranic interpretations that deny the divinity of Jesus are enhanced by the explanations or teachings of the interpreters of the Quran. It is evident that these explanations by the interpreters contradict the Quran itself.

Here, I will provide an example of a verse within the Quran that is often used to deny the divinity of Jesus or the Holy Trinity. I will present four (4) Swahili translations of this verse to show how Islamic scholars struggle to conceal the divinity of Jesus. The verse is Surah 4:171.

Translation by Aliy Muhsin Barwaani (Sunni):
"O People of the Scripture! Do not commit excess in your religion or say about Allah except the truth. The Messiah, Jesus, the son of Mary, was but a Messenger of Allah and His Word which He directed to Mary and a soul (created at a command) from Him. So believe in Allah and His messengers. And do not say, 'Three'; desist—it is better for you. Indeed, Allah is but one God. Exalted is He above having a son. To Him belongs whatever is in the heavens and whatever is on the earth. And sufficient is Allah as Disposer of affairs."

The Holy Quran (Along with Translation and Commentary in Swahili) (Ahmadiyya):
(O here it is made verse 172)
"O People of the Scripture! Do not exceed the limits in your religion, nor say about Allah except the truth. The Messiah, Jesus, the son of Mary, was but a Messenger of Allah and His Word which He directed to Mary and a soul (created at a command) from Him. So believe in Allah and His messengers. And do not say, 'Three'; desist—it is better for you: for Allah is only one God. Far exalted is He above having a son. To Him belongs all that is in the heavens and all that is on the earth. And Allah is sufficient as a Disposer of affairs."

Translation by Ali bin Jumaa bin Mayunga (Shia):

"O People of the Scripture! Do not exceed the limits in your religion, nor say about Allah except the truth. The Messiah, Jesus, the son of Mary, was but a Messenger of Allah and His Word which He directed to Mary and a soul (created at a command) from Him. So believe in Allah and His messengers. And do not say, 'Three'; desist—it is better for you. Indeed, Allah is only one God. Exalted is He above having a son. To Him belongs all that is in the heavens and all that is on the earth, and Allah is sufficient as a Disposer of affairs."

Translation by Abdallah Farsy (Sunni):
"O People of the Scripture! Do not exceed the limits in your religion, nor say about Allah except the truth. The Messiah, Jesus, the son of Mary, was but a Messenger of Allah and (a creature created by) His command (of Allah) which He directed to Mary, and a soul (created at a command) from Him (Allah like any other soul). So believe in Allah and His messengers. And do not say, 'Three'; desist (from that belief); it will be better for you. For Allah is only one God. Exalted is He above having a son. To Him belongs all that is in the heavens and all that is on the earth, and Allah is sufficient as a Disposer of affairs."

Analysis of These Translations:

I have brought this verse in different translations of the Quran to illustrate the intended meaning of this verse. When you carefully read the translation by Sheikh Balwaniy, you will find that this verse informs us of three attributes of Prophet Jesus (Isa), namely:
1. Prophet Jesus is a Messenger of Allah (meaning he was sent by God).

2. Prophet Jesus is the Word from Allah directed to Mary.
3. Prophet Jesus is a soul from Allah.

The attribute of being sent by God the Father.
The attribute that Jesus is the Word from God the Father.
The attribute that Jesus is the Spirit of God.

These three attributes of Jesus are not denied by the Holy Bible as follows:
"For God so loved the world that he gave his one and only Son, that whoever believes in him shall not perish but have eternal life. For God did not send his Son into the world to condemn the world, but to save the world through him" (John 3:16-17).

"The Word became flesh and made his dwelling among us. We have seen his glory, the glory of the one and only Son, who came from the Father, full of grace and truth" (John 1:14).

"God is spirit, and his worshipers must worship in the Spirit and in truth" (John 4:24).

It is impossible to separate God from His Spirit and His Word. If God is Spirit, then it is correct to say that the Word is also Spirit.

All three translations of the Quran I presented here—Sheikh Balwaniy, Ahmadiyya, and Mayunga—agree in the explanation of this verse. These three translators have translated word for word from Arabic in this Surah 4:171. Now let's also examine the translation of Sheikh Abdallah Farsy.

"O People of the Scripture! Do not exceed the limits in your religion, nor say about Allah except the truth. The Messiah, Jesus, the son of Mary, was but a Messenger of Allah and (a creature created by) His command (of Allah) which He directed to Mary, and a soul (created at a command) from Him (Allah like any other soul). So believe in Allah and His messengers. And do not say, 'Three'; desist (from that belief); it will be better for you. For Allah is only one God. Exalted is He above having a son. To Him belongs all that is in the heavens and all that is on the earth, and Allah is sufficient as a Disposer of affairs."

At first glance, when you analyze this translation, you will find that Sheikh Abdallah Farsy plays a word game. All the words he placed in parentheses ( ) are his additions to guide the reader to understand what he wants it to be. You will find that this translation is intentionally made to protect the Islamic belief that Allah is one, He neither begets nor is He begotten.

"(Saying: 'He is Allah, [who is] One. Allah, the Eternal Refuge. He neither begets nor is born, nor is there to Him any equivalent')" (Surah 112:1-4, Al-Ikhlas).

This Surah is the most important Surah in the Quran for Muslims. It seems that from childhood, they are required to memorize this Surah. The first pillar in Islam is the Shahada, which is to testify that "There is no god but Allah, and Muhammad is His Messenger."
It seems that the entire Islamic system is built on denying the concept of the Holy Trinity.

Unfortunately, Muslims oppose this without having a thorough understanding of this concept of the Holy Trinity. Sometimes they have created a belief that does not even exist among Christians themselves and implanted it in their followers, making Christians appear as they are not, i.e., that Christians believe in three gods.

As we have seen in this study, this belief is entirely contrary to Christianity; Christians do not believe in three gods, and this teaching is not from the Bible, but Christians believe in one God who exists in Three Living Persons, and this is what we call the HOLY TRINITY.

Let's return to the translation of Abdallah Farsy. Let's look at these words he placed in parentheses ( ).

"The Messiah, Jesus, the son of Mary, was but a Messenger of Allah and (a creature created by) His command (of Allah) which He directed to Mary."

Abdallah Farsy here is creating his own sentence by mixing the words of the Noble Quran to call them the Words of Allah. These words mean something completely different from the words of the Quran, which are:
"The Messiah, Jesus, the son of Mary, was but a Messenger of Allah

 and His Word which He directed to Mary, and a soul from Him."

He continues to add his words to distort the translation by saying:
"And a soul from Him (Allah like any other soul)."

Abdallah Farsy wants us to understand here that there are other souls that have come from Allah, so it is not surprising for Prophet Isa. In other words, this Sheikh wants to teach us that God has a "store" or warehouse of human souls which He releases and implants in humans. These words he placed in parentheses are not in the Arabic language in that verse, which is why you will find that the Sheikhs who translated word for word did not include those words.

As in the Bible, the word itself, the Holy Trinity, does not appear in the entire Quran, but by carefully examining the Bible and the Quran, we can see that this concept of the Holy Trinity is a teaching of the Holy Books. Both books agree that there is One Unique God who has no partner in all His works, and He exists in Three Living Persons of His operation: God, the Word of God, and the Holy Spirit of God. When it came time to redeem humanity, the Word became flesh, and thus we receive the titles of these Three Persons of God, namely, God the Father, God the Son, and God the Holy Spirit.

CHAPTER 07

WHO IS THE HOLY SPIRIT IN THE BIBLE AND THE QURAN?

The holy scriptures emphasize the oneness of Almighty God, declaring that He has no partner or equal. The Quran states:

"Say: He is Allah, the One and Only; Allah, the Self-Sufficient Master, Whom all creatures need. He neither begets nor is born, nor is there to Him any equivalent." *(Surah 112:1-3)*

Similarly, the Bible affirms this monotheistic belief: **"Hear, O Israel: The LORD our God, the LORD is one."** *(Deuteronomy 6:4)*

The concept of three gods or a trinity is strongly rejected in the holy scriptures. For example, the Quran says: **"They have certainly disbelieved who say, 'Allah is the**

third of three.' And there is no god except one God. And if they do not desist from what they are saying, there will surely afflict the disbelievers among them a painful punishment."
(Surah 5:73)

The Quran also warns Christians against attributing partners to God: **"O People of the Scripture, do not commit excess in your religion or say about Allah except the truth. The Messiah, Jesus, the son of Mary, was but a messenger of Allah and His word which He directed to Mary and a soul [created at a command] from Him. So believe in Allah and His messengers. And do not say, 'Three'; desist—it is better for you. Indeed, Allah is but one God. Exalted is He above having a son. To Him belongs whatever is in the heavens and whatever is on the earth. And sufficient is Allah as Disposer of affairs."** *(Surah 4:171)*

Understanding God's Oneness

The uniqueness of God is beyond question in both the Bible and the Quran. The core issue, however, lies in understanding the nature of this oneness. Both scriptures provide profound explanations of God's nature.

For instance, in the Bible, 1 John 5:8 states: **"For there are three that bear witness in heaven: the Father, the Word, and the Holy Spirit; and these three are one."**

This verse highlights the concept of unity within the Trinity, implying that God's oneness is realized through the Father, the Word (Jesus), and the Holy Spirit.

Similarly, in **Genesis 1:26**, during creation, God speaks: **"Then God said, 'Let Us make man in Our image, according to Our likeness.'"**

The use of plural pronouns ("Us" and "Our") suggests that God's oneness is not like the human understanding of singularity but encompasses a unity of persons within the divine nature.

Reflections in the Quran

The Quran also employs plural pronouns in some verses, such as: **"And We created man from sounding clay, from mud molded into shape."** *(Surah 15:26)*

"We did not create the heavens and the earth and everything between them except with truth and for a specified term." *(Surah 46:3)*

Islamic scholars often explain such plural expressions as a form of majesty rather than an indication of multiple persons. However, further analysis within the scriptures suggests otherwise.

The Role of the Holy Spirit

In the Bible, the Holy Spirit is depicted as present and active during creation: **"And the Spirit of God was hovering over the waters."** *(Genesis 1:2)*

Thus, during creation, God was accompanied by His Spirit. The Bible also describes the Holy Spirit as the one who overshadowed Mary at the birth of Jesus: **"The Holy Spirit will come upon you, and the power of the Most High will overshadow you..."** *(Luke 1:35)*

When Jesus began His ministry, He affirmed the role of the Spirit in His work, further clarifying the identity and function of the Holy Spirit.

This exploration reveals that both the Bible and the Quran highlight the greatness of God's oneness. However, the Bible provides a deeper understanding of this unity as inclusive of the Father, the Word (Jesus), and the Holy Spirit.

The Holy Spirit Speaks

The ability to speak is a characteristic of a living being, not an inanimate force or power as some might claim. For instance, the Bible records:

"The Spirit told Philip, 'Go to that chariot and stay near it.'"
(Acts 8:29)

"Now there was a man in Jerusalem called Simeon, who was righteous and devout. He was waiting for the consolation of Israel, and the Holy Spirit was on him. It had been revealed to him by the Holy Spirit that he would not die before he had seen the Lord's Messiah." *(Luke 2:25)*

"For the Holy Spirit will teach you at that time what you should say." *(Luke 12:12)*

These verses (emphasis mine) illustrate that the Holy Spirit is a living being capable of communication, not merely a force or power.

Islamic Perspective on the Holy Spirit

Islamic scholars often associate the "Spirit of God" with Prophet Muhammad. For example, they interpret **John 16:13** as a prophecy about Muhammad:

"But when He, the Spirit of truth, comes, He will guide you into all the truth. He will not speak on His own; He will speak only what He hears, and He will tell you what is yet to come."

Muslims believe this verse foretells the coming of Prophet Muhammad (peace be upon him). However, when we examine the characteristics of the Holy Spirit, it becomes clear that this cannot refer to Muhammad.

Characteristics of the Holy Spirit

1. **Present at Creation: "In the beginning, God created the heavens and the earth. Now the Spirit of God was hovering over the waters."** *(Genesis 1:1)*
2. **Present in Noah's Time: "My Spirit will not contend with humans forever, for they are mortal."** *(Genesis 6:3)*
3. **Present during Moses' Time: "Yet they rebelled and grieved His Holy Spirit. So He turned and became their enemy and He Himself fought against them."** *(Isaiah 63:10)*
4. **Strengthens Prophets and Intercedes:** The Holy Spirit empowers God's messengers and serves as an intercessor for believers.

The Holy Spirit Is Not Muhammad

The attributes of the Holy Spirit exclude Muhammad from being identified as the Spirit of God. Muhammad was never intended to be an intercessor for believers. On the contrary, Islamic teachings instruct believers to pray for Muhammad. For example, the Quran states:

"Indeed, Allah and His angels send blessings upon the Prophet. O you who have believed, ask [Allah to confer] blessing upon him and ask [Allah to grant him] peace." *(Surah 33:56)*

This verse shows that even Muhammad relies on the prayers of believers and the blessings of Allah. Muslims, upon mentioning Muhammad's name, say, **"Sallallahu alayhi wa sallam"** (May Allah's blessings and peace be upon him).

If Allah is unique and peerless, as both the Bible and Quran affirm, it raises the question: How can Allah "pray" for Muhammad? This suggests a relationship among distinct persons within the divine nature, as seen in the Christian doctrine of the Trinity, where one divine person may intercede for another.

The Trinity and Intercession

The concept of the Trinity explains how one person of the Godhead can pray or intercede for another. For example, the Holy Spirit is described as an advocate or intercessor for the saints. The unique nature of God, as revealed in the Bible, encompasses three persons—Father, Son, and Holy Spirit—united in essence yet distinct in function.

In conclusion, attributing the role of the Holy Spirit to Muhammad is inconsistent with the scriptural evidence. Instead, the Holy Spirit is a living, active person of the divine Godhead with unique roles and functions distinct from any human prophet, including Muhammad.

Who is the Holy Spirit in the Quran?

As seen in the Bible, Almighty God strengthened the Prophet Isa (Jesus) with the Holy Spirit, enabling him to perform many miracles.

"We gave Moses the Book and followed him up with a succession of messengers. We gave Jesus, son of Mary, clear signs and strengthened him with the Holy Spirit. Whenever a messenger came to you with what you did not desire, you became arrogant, rejecting some and killing others." *(Surah 2:87)*

"And [mention] when Allah will say, 'O Jesus, son of Mary, remember My favor upon you and upon your mother when I strengthened you with the Holy Spirit to speak to people in childhood and maturity, and when I taught you the Scripture and wisdom and the Torah and the Gospel, and when you designed from clay what was like the form of a bird with My permission, then you breathed into it, and it became a bird with My permission, and you healed the blind and the lepers with My permission, and when you brought forth the dead with My permission, and when I restrained the Children of Israel from [harming] you when you came to them with clear proofs.'" *(Surah 5:110)*

Muslim Interpretation of the Holy Spirit

To avoid the concept of the Trinity in the Quran, Muslims often claim that the "Holy Spirit" mentioned in these verses refers to the Angel Jibril (Gabriel). However, when asked for Quranic evidence supporting the claim that the Holy

Spirit is Jibril, no direct answer can be found. This association is based on an assumption rather than a clear statement in the Quran.

Two Quranic verses are commonly cited to support this claim:

1. **"Say, 'Whoever is an enemy to Gabriel—it is [none but] he who has brought the Quran down upon your heart, [O Muhammad], by permission of Allah, confirming that which was before it and as guidance and good tidings for the believers.'"**
   (Surah 2:97)
2. **"Say, 'The Holy Spirit has brought it down from your Lord in truth to make firm those who believe and as guidance and good tidings to the Muslims.'"**
   (Surah 16:102)

From these verses, some Muslims conclude:

- Since Surah 2:97 states that Jibril brought the Quran, and
- Surah 16:102 states that the Holy Spirit brought the Quran,
- Therefore, Jibril must be the Holy Spirit.

This reasoning is flawed. Nowhere in the Quran does it explicitly state that "Jibril is the Holy Spirit." Neither does any hadith clearly identify Jibril as the Holy Spirit.

A Deeper Look into Revelation (Wahy)

Islamic scholars explain that revelation was delivered to Prophet Muhammad (peace be upon him) through various means. According to the book *Ar-Raheeq Al-Makhtum* (The Sealed Nectar), page 109, the stages of revelation included:

1. **True dreams:** The initial phase of revelation.
2. **Inspiration placed in the Prophet's heart and mind:** Without visible manifestation.
3. **Appearance of an angel in human form:** The angel would speak directly to the Prophet.
4. **Revelation like the ringing of a bell:** The most intense form of revelation.
5. **Seeing the angel in his true form.**
6. **Direct words of Allah.**

These methods show that revelation was not delivered through a single channel, and conflating different verses about revelation delivery overlooks the Prophet's own accounts of how revelation occurred.

The Role of the Holy Spirit in Revelation

Re-reading **Surah 16:102** without preconceived interpretations or external commentaries reveals: **"Say, 'The Holy Spirit has brought it down from your Lord in truth to strengthen those who believe and as guidance and good tidings to the Muslims.'"**

The verse does not mention Jibril at all. It simply states that the Holy Spirit brought the Quran. Associating Jibril with the Holy Spirit here is an extrapolation, not an explicit statement from the Quran.

Conclusion

The Quran itself does not identify Jibril as the Holy Spirit. Instead, the interpretation linking the two is based on Islamic tradition and commentary rather than clear textual evidence. Furthermore, the characteristics of the Holy Spirit as described in both the Quran and the Bible suggest a unique role that goes beyond the angelic function traditionally attributed to Jibril.

The deeper theological implications of the Holy Spirit's role in the Quran, particularly when compared to its role in the Bible, merit further discussion and reflection.

Who is the Spirit of Truth According to the Holy Scriptures?

Muslims claim that Prophet Muhammad is foretold in the Bible as the Spirit of Truth. They argue that there is the Holy Spirit and the Spirit of Truth, suggesting that these are two distinct entities. Surprisingly, this interpretation implies that the Spirit of Truth is not holy. This leads to the question: if the Spirit of Truth is not holy, does that make it unclean? For holiness is the opposite of impurity.

According to the Holy Scriptures, any Spirit from God is both holy and true. The Spirit is referred to as the Spirit of Truth to distinguish it from the deceptive spirits of demons described in the Bible:

- "The Spirit clearly says that in later times some will abandon the faith and follow deceiving spirits and things taught by demons." (1 Timothy 4:1)
- "Then I saw three impure spirits that looked like frogs; they came out of the mouth of the dragon, out of the mouth of the beast, and out of the mouth of the false prophet. They are demonic spirits…" (Revelation 16:13-14)

Jesus called the Holy Spirit the Spirit of Truth to differentiate it from these false spirits that deceive people of faith in our times. Let us examine the verse Muslims often use to claim it refers to Muhammad:

"But very truly I tell you, it is for your good that I am going away. Unless I go away, the Advocate will not come to you; but if I go, I will send him to you. When he comes, he will prove the world to be in the wrong about sin and righteousness and judgment: about sin, because people do not believe in me; about righteousness, because I am going to the Father, where you can see me no longer; and about judgment, because the prince of this world now stands condemned. I have much more to say to you, more than you can now bear. But when he, the Spirit of Truth, comes, he will guide you into all the truth. He will not speak on his own; he will speak only what he hears, and he will tell you what is yet to come. He will glorify me because it is from me that he will

receive what he will make known to you. All that belongs to the Father is mine. That is why I said the Spirit will receive from me what he will make known to you." (John 16:7-15)

Muslims argue that this passage refers to Muhammad because:

1. **The Spirit of Truth will prove the world wrong about sin**—they claim Muhammad established Islam, warning people about sin and evil.
2. **The Spirit of Truth will prove the world wrong about righteousness**—they argue that Muhammad taught a religion of righteousness.
3. **The Spirit of Truth will prove the world wrong about judgment**—they assert that Muhammad instituted Islamic laws and judgments.

To test these claims, let us examine whether the characteristics of the Spirit of Truth as described by Jesus align with Muhammad.

Characteristics of the Spirit of Truth According to Jesus

1. **The Spirit of Truth is called the Advocate and comes to those who love Jesus and keep His commandments** (John 14:15-16).
   - Question: Do Muslims love Jesus and keep His commandments?
2. **The Spirit of Truth will dwell with believers forever** (John 14:16).
   - Question: Does Muhammad dwell with Muslims forever? No. Muhammad passed

away on Monday, June 8, 632 CE, over 1,400 years ago. (Source: Abdallah Farsy, *The Life of Prophet Muhammad*, p. 81).

3. **The Spirit of Truth is unseen by the world and known only to believers** (John 14:17).
   - Question: Was Muhammad invisible to non-believers? No. Muhammad was seen by his opponents, and he even engaged in battles with them.

These characteristics clearly do not align with Muhammad. Instead, they describe the Holy Spirit, who dwells in the hearts of believers, guiding them in truth and glorifying Christ.

How Does the Holy Spirit Convict the World About Sin, Righteousness, and Judgment?

We have already established that the prophets of God speak messages from Him, guided by the Holy Spirit:

- "For prophecy never had its origin in the human will, but prophets, though human, spoke from God as they were carried along by the Holy Spirit." (2 Peter 1:21)
- "It was revealed to them that they were not serving themselves but you, when they spoke of the things that have now been told you by those who have preached the gospel to you by the Holy Spirit sent from heaven." (1 Peter 1:11)

Thus, when servants of God preach, rebuke sin, and warn people about the coming judgment, the Holy Spirit works through them to accomplish this.

- "Now to each one the manifestation of the Spirit is given for the common good. To one there is given through the Spirit a message of wisdom, to another a message of knowledge by means of the same Spirit, to another faith by the same Spirit, to another gifts of healing by that one Spirit, to another miraculous powers, to another prophecy, to another distinguishing between spirits, to another speaking in different kinds of tongues, and to still another the interpretation of tongues. All these are the work of one and the same Spirit, and he distributes them to each one, just as he determines." (1 Corinthians 12:7-11)

God is one, but His unity is not like anything the human mind can fully grasp. God is one in being, yet He exists in three living Persons. This unique Trinity is unlike anything or anyone else. Therefore, God declares that He has no equal. No other god or gods can possess His nature, being one God while existing as three living Persons.

The Qur'an and the Rejection of the Trinity

The Qur'an rejects the concept of the Trinity, but it is essential to understand the context. The Qur'an critiques the polytheistic practices of the Quraysh tribe in Mecca, who worshiped three deities represented by idols. Muhammad prohibited this pagan religion and instructed people not to liken Allah to these idols.

The Qur'an states:

- "Have you considered al-Lat, al-Uzza, and Manat, the third one? Should you have sons while He has daughters? This is indeed an unfair division." (Surah 53:19-22)

Here, Muhammad critiques the claim that these pagan gods had daughters while humans had sons, labeling such a belief unjust.

Further, the Qur'an adds:

- "These are but [mere] names you have named them— you and your forefathers— for which Allah has sent down no authority. They follow nothing but assumptions and what their souls desire, while guidance has already come to them from their Lord." (Surah 53:23)

These verses directly address the idols al-Lat, al-Uzza, and Manat, the three deities worshiped by the polytheists in Mecca. It is clear that the Qur'an opposes the pagan concept of three gods. However, this does not align with the Christian doctrine of the Trinity.

The Trinity in Christianity

In contrast, Christians do not worship three gods. The Bible teaches that God is one, yet He exists as three living Persons: the Father, the Son, and the Holy Spirit. This unique unity is distinct from the pagan understanding of three separate gods. No part of the Bible supports the worship of multiple gods. Instead, it proclaims:

- "Hear, O Israel: The Lord our God, the Lord is one." (Deuteronomy 6:4)
- "Therefore go and make disciples of all nations, baptizing them in the name of the Father and of the Son and of the Holy Spirit." (Matthew 28:19)

The Trinity is a mystery, but it underscores God's unique nature and divine essence, which no created being or belief system can replicate.

www.ingramcontent.com/pod-product-compliance
Lightning Source LLC
Chambersburg PA
CBHW070811170726
48000CB00017B/634